An Introduction to
Sixteenth-Century
Counterpoint
and Palestrina's
Musical Style

Robert Stewart

dsley House Publishers, Inc. ■ New York

Address orders and editorial
correspondence to:
Ardsley House, Publishers, Inc.
320 Central Park West
New York, NY 10025

ISBN: 1-880157-07-1

Printed in the United States of America

10 9 8 7 6 5 4 3 2 1

To My Students

Contents

Chapter 1
Basic Materials and Melodic Writing *1*

Chapter 2
Counterpoint in Two Parts   22

Chapter 3
Counterpoint in Three Parts   49

Chapter 4
Counterpoint in Four and Five Parts   65

Appendix A
Examples for Musical Analysis   75

Appendix B
Written Exercises   187

Preface

The purpose of this text is to present a basic, systematic approach to polyphonic composition in the ecclesiastical style of Palestrina. Beginning with the principles of melodic structure and concentrating on two- and three-part writing, the study concludes with a brief discussion of four- and five-voiced composition. Since this text is designed for use in beginning- and intermediate-level courses in modal counterpoint, a discussion of advanced polyphonic composition employing parody, paraphrase, and *cantus firmus* techniques is not included.

Chapter 1 has been subdivided into five sections to facilitate the presentation of materials in self-contained, discrete units. Although the arrangement of this material is based on the expectation that melodic writing will begin after Section 1.3 (Notation and Guidelines), the sequence of sections may be assigned in any number of configurations to suit the individual pedagogical needs of the instructor. For example, should the instructor wish to introduce text setting before specific melodic idioms, the sequence of sections would be: 1.1, 1.2, 1.5, 1.3, 1.4; or, should it be deemed more desirable to delay melodic composition until all characteristics have been covered, the sequence 1.1, 1.2, 1.4, 1.3, 1.5 would be used.

Chapter 2 considers writing two-part counterpoint, white-note dissonances, and the treatment of black-note idioms, and concludes with a discussion of writing invertible counterpoint. Chapter 3, which is similar to Chapter 2 in organization and presentation of materials, covers three-part counterpoint, concluding with a discussion of the consonant fourth and the six-five chord. Chapter 4, which is basically an extension of Chapter 3, deals primarily with problems of texture, voice doubling in chords, cadences, and triple meter. The written exercises in Appendix II (W-11 through W-15), which are intended to accompany Chapter 4, were designed to offer students several methods for writing multiple-voiced counterpoint within the context of the discussion set forth in this chapter.

Appendix A includes two-part works from Lassus' *Cantiones duarum vocum* and a comprehensive collection of works by

Palestrina. This collection is drawn from the composer's hymns, Lamentations, Litanies, Magnificats, Masses, motets, and Offertories, including examples in three to five parts. The three-part works are arranged to parallel the presentation of stylistic devices in Chapter 3, with the technically simpler works followed progressively by those dealing with more advanced techniques, the concluding measures of *Vetustam fecit* not withstanding!

Appendix B contains exercises designed to be used in conjunction with this text. If these exercises are used on a regular basis, they should prove sufficient in developing basic written skills. In classes that emphasize writing over analysis, however, they will function more successfully when used as supplemental material to an instructor's usual written exercises.

Although most of the stylistic elements found in Palestrina's music are dealt with in depth, an introductory text, by its very nature, must exclude those characteristics that are unusual or are rarely found. For this reason, daily analysis of Palestrina's music will prove useful not only as a means of correcting the distorted understanding that results from dealing in stylistic generalities, but also as an important aid to the student in achieving stylisic comprehension.

By focusing this study on Palestrina's contrapuntal style, the student will more easily develop a systematic and reliable method with which to compare and synthesize the many other stylistic trends that developed during the Renaissance. As a result, the unique musical qualities and characteristics of individual composers will become more clearly evident, easily comprehended and, it is hoped, more deeply appreciated.

Before beginning this study, some preliminary reading by the student is highly recommended. A reference text such as *The New Harvard Dictionary of Music*, edited by Don Randel, should be consulted for a discussion of the following terms: Clef, Counterpoint, Bar line, Gregorian chant, Mass, Mensural notation, Mode, *Musica ficta*, *Musica reservata*, Notation, Species counterpoint, and Tactus.

Acknowledgments

I wish to express my appreciation and gratitude to Dr. Gary Maas, Ms. Sue Okuda, and Ms. Barbara Hove for their unique contribution to the preparation of this text. I would also like to thank Laura Jones and Dena Wallenstein of Ardsley House for their creative and professional contributions in the preparation of my manuscript for publication.

An Introduction to

Sixteenth-Century

Counterpoint

and Palestrina's

Musical Style

1 Basic Materials and Melodic Writing

1.1 BASIC MATERIALS

Ecclesiastical (Church) Modes

Early chant (plainsong) was based on scale formations called **modes**. Of the original eight modes, four were designated as **authentic** and four as **plagal**. Plagal and authentic modes occur in pairs that share the same final (the note on which the mode is based), but differ in range and recitation tones (dominants). Plagal forms use the prefix *Hypo*; therefore, Dorian (with a range of d to d[1] and a dominant on pitch class a) is an authentic mode and Hypodorian (with a range of A to a, and a dominant on pitch class f) is the plagal form, with both using the same final (d).[1]

By the sixteenth century, the original eight modes were expanded to include four additional forms (recognized by Glareanus in his *Dodekachordon*, 1547): Aeolian, Hypoaeolian, Ionian, and Hypoionian, resulting in a total of twelve modes. The Locrian (range B to b) and the Hypolocrian modes were recognized by theorists, but never used by composers. Notice also that pitch class B is never used as a dominant in any of the modes.

---

[1]The mode of a particular chant is determined by its final and its ambitus (melodic range). When the range of a chant extends more or less from final to final, it is considered to be in an authentic mode. A chant whose range extends more or less from dominant to dominant is considered to be in a plagal mode.

EXAMPLE *1.1*   THE AUTHENTIC AND PLAGAL MODES

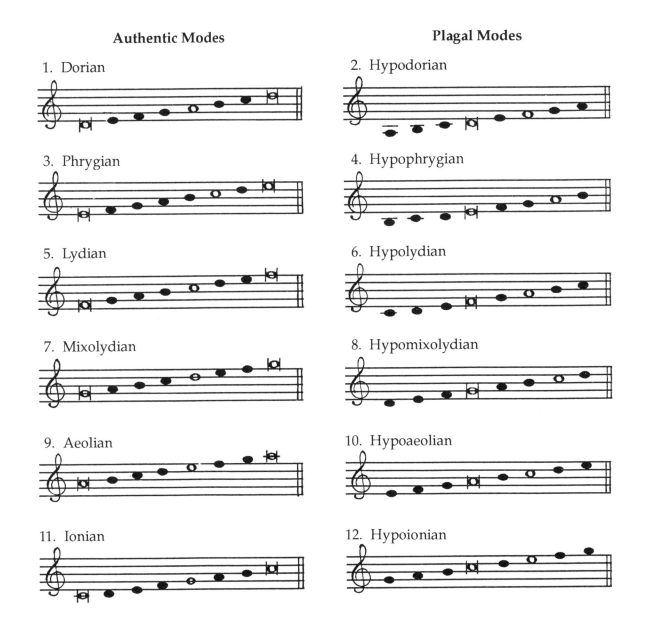

Transposition   The modes were often transposed up a fourth (or down a fifth), requiring the use of B♭ in the "key" signature. Numerous musical examples using this transposition can be found in Appendix I.

Notation and Rhythm   Our modern notation system is the product of many years of development and refinement. As a result of this continuous change, much of our musical heritage must be transcribed into modern notation for performance and study.

During the 16th century, voice parts were usually printed separately in partbooks (i.e., separate books for Cantus, Altus, etc.). These parts were notated with diamond-shaped notes (◇, ◈, ◆, etc.); they primarily used the C and F clefs, lacked bar lines, and used symbols such as ₵, 0, and ∅ to indicate meter. In modern transcriptions the meter signature $\frac{4}{2}$ is used interchangeably with the ₵ symbol to denote duple meter. In each measure of $\frac{4}{2}$ time, notes falling on beats 1 and 3 are treated as primary or accented beats. Notes falling on beats 2 and 4 are treated as secondary or unaccented beats.

EXAMPLE 1.2   METRIC PULSE

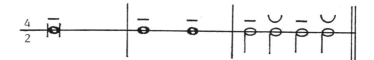

Rhythmic contrast in this style was not created through syncopated subdivisions of the beat, as found in most modern music, but by means of agogic accents (created by the use of longer note duration), accented syllables occurring on secondary beats (2 and 4), the use of contrasting sections in triple meter, and, somewhat, by harmonic factors. In discussions about rhythm, it is well to remember that the flow of music through time is constantly being shaped by the interaction of rhythm, meter, and tempo in combination and, although each is treated separately, their combined effect is that of a single unit. Despite the fact that there is some uncertainty regarding tempo in this style, most sources agree on a general range of ○ = M.M. 48–69.

The following note values (shown in modern notation) were used in ecclesiastical polyphonic compositions written in $\frac{4}{2}$ meter during the Renaissance.

EXAMPLE 1.3   NOTE DURATIONS (ADJACENT NOTE VALUES ARE IN A 2:1 RATIO)

◙	Breve	(Double whole note)
○	Semibreve	(Whole note)
♩	Minim	(Half note)
♩	Semiminim	(Quarter note)
♪	Fusa	(Eighth note)

The maxima ▭ (equals ◙ X 4) and the longa ▭ (equals ◙ X 2) were also used, although, they tend to occur with less frequency than do the durations listed in Example 1.3.

Rests equivalent to white-note values are the only type commonly found in this style.[2] Notice that rests are placed in the third space of the staff regardless of the clef being used.

EXAMPLE 1.4   **AVAILABLE RESTS**

Due to the lack of bar lines in this music, note values were lengthened by means of dots rather than through the use of ties. The dot following a note is equal to one-half the value of that note $\left(\mathbf{o}\cdot = \mathbf{o} + \mathit{d}\ \text{or}\ \mathbf{o}\ \mathit{d}\right)$. Dots were usually added to white notes only and, consequently, excluded certain possibilities (for example, $\mathbf{o}\ \mathit{d}$) because they are impossible to achieve through the use of dots. This practice, in addition to the use of bar lines, dictates that ties be used in the following restricted manner:

1. The initial note of a tie must always be a white-note value.

2. A tie may be made either to a note of equal value or to a note of one-half its value. The exception $\mathbf{o}\ \_\ \mathbf{\lvert o\rvert}\ \Vert$ may be used at the end of large sections or movements on occasion.

3. Larger note values (breves, dotted breves, and dotted whole notes) must occur on beats 1 and 3 only.

4. Dotted notes, for the present, must never be tied (Example 1.6).

EXAMPLE 1.5   **TIES**

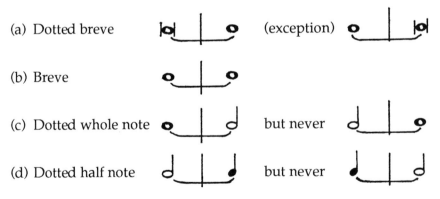

(a) Dotted breve   (exception)

(b) Breve

(c) Dotted whole note   but never

(d) Dotted half note   but never

---

[2]Given the acoustical properties of the average cathedral, shorter rests would most likely be neutralized through natural reverberation and therefore would be impractical.

Illustrations (a), (b), and (c) occur on beats 1 or 3 only; illustration (d), the dotted half note, may occur on any beat. Although tied dotted notes are found in triple meter, in $\frac{4}{2}$ meter *none* of the following are acceptable.

EXAMPLE 1.6 UNACCEPTABLE TIES

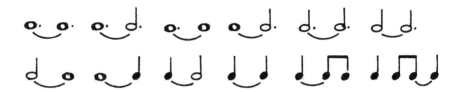

1.2 MELODIC WRITING

Melodic Structure Choral parts and solo song are usually compared and judged separately because melodies functioning in a polyphonic web must adhere to certain rhythmic and melodic restraints not necessarily applied to solo song. However, by incorporating secular song in their sacred music, Renaissance composers tended to mediate and minimize these inherent differences. Note the similarities and differences in the melodies of Example 1.7 on page 6. The first, *L'Homme armé* (*The Armed Man*), was a popular secular song of Palestrina's time; the second, the Cantus from the *Kyrie* section of Palestrina's Missa: *L'Homme armé* (see Appendix I, page 155).

Formally, Palestrina's melody is asymmetrical, lacking the balanced ABA structure of *L'Homme armé*. Also, while the solo song has a forceful individuality of its own, Palestrina's related melody is more ornate and subtle rhythmically. In addition to the rhythmic structure, notice that stepwise movement predominates and that except for the skip of a third, all single and double skips are preceded and followed by stepwise movement in contrary direction. Finally, the overall distribution of note values should be observed. Polyphonic sacred music of the 16th century invariably began with long note values, gradually went into shorter values, then returned to longer values at cadence points.

The following guidelines and examples will be of help when writing melodies in Palestrina's style. Do not become discouraged when exceptions to these guidelines are found in the music in Appendix I. These exceptions do not invalidate rules that are based on commonly used musical procedures. Exceptions do, however, provide subtle information about a composer's origi-

EXAMPLE 1.7   **(a) L'HOMME ARMÉ (ANON.)**
(b) CANTUS FROM THE KYRIE SECTION OF
Missa: L'HOMME ARMÉ, Palestrina

(a) L'Homme armé

D. C. al 𝄐

(b) Cantus

nality and his mastery of writing in a given style, and should be carefully studied for these reasons. The main point the author wishes to make is that, in order to write convincingly in any given style, it is just as necessary to avoid certain musical procedures as it is to exploit others.

Melodic Intervals   The melodic style of Palestrina is based primarily on conjunct melodic movement. Therefore, it is best to consider stepwise movement as the norm and to treat skips as a controlled aspect of contrast. Skips of a third and fourth should be used more frequently than larger skips, and the *minor* sixth should be used in *ascending* direction only.

EXAMPLE 1.8   MELODIC INTERVALS (ASCENDING ↑ AND DESCENDING ↓)

Commonly used intervals:

Major and minor thirds	(↑ ↓)
Perfect fourth	(↑ ↓)
Perfect fifth	(↑ ↓)
Perfect octave	(↑); less frequently (↓)
Minor sixth	(↑) only

The following were not used:

Major sixth
Major and minor sevenths
All augmented and diminished steps or skips

Chromatic Alteration (*Musica Ficta*)

During the Renaissance many composers were drawn to the study and use of chromaticism as an extension and enrichment of musical expression. Works of exceptional beauty (as well as musical curiosity) were written by Vicentino, Rore, Lassus, and Gesualdo, among others. This stylistically advanced music contrasts sharply with the conservative, diatonically based music of Palestrina and other composers of the Roman school.

What helps to make the study of Renaissance music so rewarding is the wide range of musical styles that coexisted and came to fruition during those years. It was not until the 20th century that such diversity in musical styles again emerged to challenge and enrich the musical environment of professionals and laymen alike.

The use of *musica ficta* (accidentals) is very restricted in the music of Palestrina; chromaticism is rarely used at all.[3] The only commonly encountered accidentals are B♭ and E♭ (used to avoid tritones[4]), and C♯, F♯, and G♯ (used to create leading tones in cadences). The following points should be observed regarding the use of *musica ficta* and the treatment of dissonant intervals in melodic writing.

1. The harmonic and melodic interval of a tritone (referred to as *diabolus in musica*) occurs diatonically in every mode between the pitches F and B (or B and F) and must be corrected with a B♭.[5]

EXAMPLE 1.9   TRITONE CORRECTION

melodic correction   harmonic correction

---

[3]In Litaniae Liber Secundus, compare the F♯ (Palestrina's ficta) in the Altus, measure 42, page 183, to the F♮ in the following measure in Tenor I.

[4]A tritone is the interval of an augmented 4th or a diminished 5th.

[5]In transposed modes, the tritone occurs between B flat and E natural and is corrected with an E flat.

2. If a melody outlines a tritone within one or two measures, it also should be corrected.

EXAMPLE 1.10   TRITONE OUTLINING

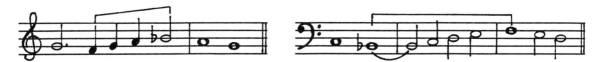

3. Except for the *minor* seventh, avoid outlining all dissonant intervals (major sevenths, ninths, or augmented and diminished intervals). Note that the use of *musica ficta*, especially at cadence points, may result in the creation of unacceptable intervals.

EXAMPLE 1.11   OUTLINING OTHER DISSONANT INTERVALS

4. Avoid all steps or skips that involve diminished or augmented intervals.

EXAMPLE 1.12   AUGMENTED AND DIMINISHED INTERVALS

5. Chromatic half steps (notes preceded or followed by their own alteration: C–C♯, B–B♭, etc.) should always be avoided. However, diatonic half steps (A–B♭, C♯–D, etc.) may be freely used for functional purposes.

EXAMPLE 1.13   CHROMATIC ALTERATION

Stepwise Movement in White Notes

There are no specific restrictions placed on the use of white-note values in stepwise movement beyond those mentioned in the preceding discussion (i.e., in regard to the use of ties, the placement of dotted breves, breves, and dotted whole notes on accented beats, and the outlining of dissonant intervals).

Single Skips in White Notes

Single skips greater than a third should be preceded and followed by stepwise movement in contrary directions. Remember that all skips are limited intervallically to those listed in Example 1.8.

EXAMPLE 1.14   ASCENDING AND DESCENDING WHITE-NOTE SKIPS

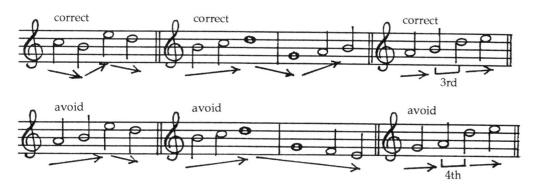

Double Skips in White Notes

Double skips should be based on triadic structure or be used to divide the leap of an octave with a perfect fourth or fifth.[6] As with single skips, double skips are normally preceded and followed by stepwise movement in contrary directions. Although double skips may occur anywhere, they are most often found at the beginning of phrases and in the bass part at cadences.

---

[6]Additional white-note skips will be illustrated in Examples 1.27 and 1.28 on page 18.

EXAMPLE 1.15   DOUBLE SKIPS IN WHITE NOTES

Idiomatic Rhythmic Patterns   The black- and white-note rhythmic patterns illustrated in Examples 16 and 17 are commonly found in this style. Carefully note those combinations that should be avoided.

EXAMPLE 1.16   COMMON RHYTHMIC PATTERNS

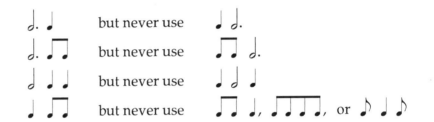

While these rhythmic patterns may frequently be encountered throughout a melodic phrase, a single pattern is rarely repeated consecutively.

EXAMPLE 1.17   CONSECUTIVE USE OF RHYTHMIC PATTERNS

Stepwise Movement in Black Notes   Quarter and eighth notes are much more restricted in usage than are white notes. Quarter notes are most often used in stepwise motion and require special caution because their use involves the off-beat.

Eighth notes occur in pairs on the *off-beat only*. They must be stepwise and must always be approached and left by step (i.e., never skip to, from, or between eighth notes).

EXAMPLE 1.18   USE OF EIGHTH NOTES

When black-note passages create an upward melodic arch, the highest note of the arch is felt as an accent. If this accented high note falls on the off-beat, it creates syncopation by emphasizing the off-beat and should be avoided. Although the high note of an *ascending* quarter-note passage must never fall on the off-beat, *descending* passages may be treated freely in this regard.

EXAMPLE 1.19   OFF-BEAT ACCENTS (OFF BEAT ↑; DOWN BEAT ↓)

Single Skips in Quarter Notes

Use *single skips only* with quarter notes. Apply the principles of contrary stepwise movement illustrated in Example 1.14, but avoid skips larger than a perfect fifth. Quarter-note skips that ascend must be made *from* an off-beat; skips that descend must be made *to* an off-beat.[7] (This rule is based on the principle illustrated in Example 1.19.)

EXAMPLE 1.20 ASCENDING AND DESCENDING QUARTER-NOTE SKIPS

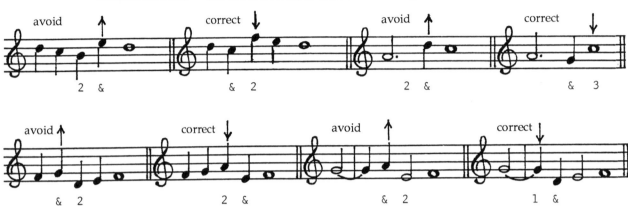

1.3 NOTATION AND GUIDELINES

Melodic Contour

The shape of a melodic phrase is determined by the arrangement of its successive high and low points. The simplest and most commonly encountered phrase structure is one in which the melodic line rises to a high point, then gradually descends for the remainder of the phrase. In the interest of achieving balance, the lowest point of a phrase is treated in a similar manner, lending a sense of ebb and flow to the melodic process. When writing melodies, use melodic skips in combination with stepwise passages that outline smaller intervals (e.g., fourths through sixths) to create melodic contours similar to the following:

---

[7]See the *nota cambiata* for an exception, but note that it is the interval of a third that is involved.

Voice Ranges Although composers of 16th century vocal music used some type of full score when composing their works, they apparently discarded them after the various parts were extracted. Consequently, most modern scores are reconstructed from existing voice parts. These realizations use the familiar treble and bass clefs; tenor parts use the double treble clef (𝄞𝄞) as a reminder and visual signal that the tenor part *sounds one octave lower than written*. In altus parts requiring this octave transposition, a treble clef with an octave sign placed at or near its base (𝄞₈) is used rather than the double treble clef.[8]

EXAMPLE 1.21 VOICE RANGES

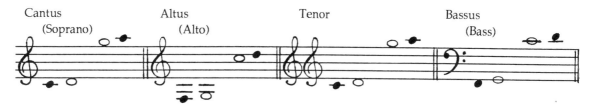

Cantus (Soprano)   Altus (Alto)   Tenor   Bassus (Bass)

Because only males were allowed to sing in sacred choirs during the Renaissance, the bassus and tenor parts were sung by men and the altus and cantus parts by young boys.

Guidelines for Writing Melodies

1. Always begin on a primary modal degree (final, dominant, or plagal dominant) with a value no less than a dotted half note.

2. Use larger note values at the beginning and gradually introduce shorter note values as the melody progresses.

3. Stepwise movement should prevail. Use frequent changes of direction and occasional skips for contrast.

4. Avoid outlining dissonant intervals; use B♭ to correct the skip to, or outline of, the tritone.

5. Strive for asymmetrical rhythmic structure by using ties and dotted notes. Avoid the consecutive repetition of similar rhythmic patterns, long passages of equal note values, and melodic sequence.

6. Do not repeat notes unless setting a text. (Refer to Example 1.25 for an exception.)

7. Always end on the final with a whole note or breve.

---

[8]In most modern choral editions, the single treble clef with attached octave sign is used exclusively for the tenor. In these editions, alto parts are never transposed and sound as written.

8. Always approach the final by step from above or below.

9. When approaching the final from below, raise the seventh scale degree to create a leading tone in the Dorian, Mixolydian, or Aeolian modes.

10. Generally, avoid the outer limits of voice ranges.

Manuscript Format

Tenor   Aeolian

1. Always label the voice part and name the mode.

2. Use a straight edge for bar lines.

3. Be sure the stem direction is up on notes below the middle line and down on notes above the middle line.

4. Ties always go opposite stems:

Phrase markings are not used in this style.

5. Copy slowly and carefully for clarity and neatness. Use a pencil with soft lead.

1.4 MELODIC IDIOMS

Single Skips Using Black- and White-Note Values   As illustrated in Example 1.22, a skip from a white-note value to a quarter-note passage is usually made from a half note. A *descending* skip should be made to an *ascending* quarter-note passage and an *ascending* skip to a *descending* passage. All suitable intervals may be used in the skip except the sixth. With the exception of a *single* skip of a third, all skips should be preceded and followed by stepwise movement in contrary direction.

EXAMPLE 1.22   SKIPS FROM HALF NOTES TO QUARTER NOTES

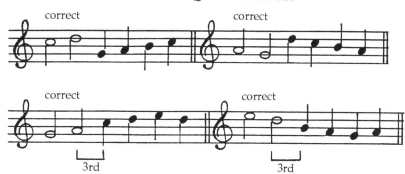

Skips from a descending quarter-note passage may ascend to any white-note value smaller than a breve. Again, use contrary stepwise motion and avoid the interval of a sixth.

EXAMPLE 1.23   SKIPS FROM DESCENDING QUARTER NOTES TO WHITE NOTES

The following illustrations are drawn from the music of Palestrina.

Double Skips Using Black- and White-Note Values

The most common double-skip figures based on black- and white-note values are illustrated in Example 1.24 (and the ensuing examples from Palestrina). These double-skip figures share the following characteristics:

1. The figure is initiated by a descending skip of a third or, less frequently, by a perfect fourth or fifth.

2. The descending quarter-note skip is followed by an ascending skip to any white-note value less than a breve.

3. These figures may occur on any beat and are usually preceded by quarter-note, half-note, or dotted half-note values.

4. Except when the interval of a third is involved, these figures are normally preceded and followed by stepwise movement in contrary direction.

EXAMPLE *1.24* **BASIC SHAPES OF THE DOUBLE-SKIP FIGURE**

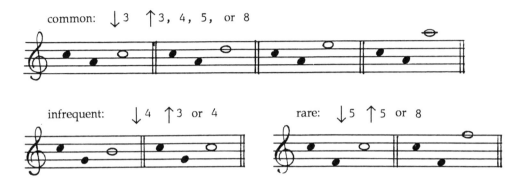

The following examples are drawn from the music of Palestrina. Carefully compare these with the basic shapes in Example 1.24.

Anticipation (*Portamento*) The anticipation is a quarter-note value that descends by step on the off-beat of 1 or 3. It is preceded by either another quarter note or by a dotted half note. Examples of ascending anticipations are rare and should be avoided.

EXAMPLE *1.25* **ANTICIPATIONS**

Nota Cambiata The cambiata is a common melodic figure found in most sacred and secular music of the Renaissance. The figure is based on the following intervallic structure:

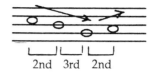

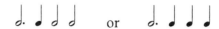

A cambiata figure may begin on any beat and any note except B natural and should be limited rhythmically to

$$ \textit{♩.}\ ♩\ ♩\ \textit{♩}\quad\text{or}\quad\textit{♩.}\ ♩\ ♩\ ♩ $$

for the present.[9]

EXAMPLE 1.26   NOTA CAMBIATA

Other Skip Patterns The two melodic figures discussed in Examples 1.27 and 1.28 share a common melodic process with the *nota cambiata*. As illustrated in the following example, a cambiata is formed when a descending stepwise movement is momentarily "interrupted" by the downward diversional skip of a third.

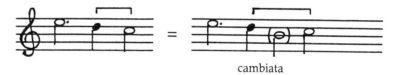

cambiata

The first related pattern also makes use of a diversional "escape tone" with a leap from, and return to, a basic stepwise movement. These figures, however, involve a return to a note a second *above* or *below* the initial pitch. They usually appear in white-note values, but if the second note is a quarter note, it must occur on the off-beat and descend. Notice that the general practice of leaving skips by stepwise movement in contrary direction is often ignored in this pattern.

[9]A rare example of the cambiata in rhythmic augmentation may be found in the Cantus and Bassus of Palestrina's motet: *Exaudi Domine*, measures 40–42, page 127.

EXAMPLE 1.27 **DIVERSIONAL SKIP PATTERNS**

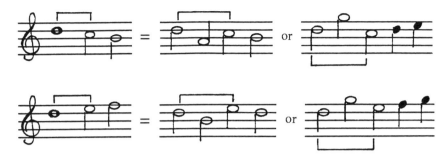

Study the following examples, all of which are drawn from the music of Palestrina.

Summary of usable skip combinations:

↓ 3   ↑ 4

↑ 4   ↓ 3   or   ↓ 5

↓ 4   ↑ 3   or   ↑ 5

↓ 5   ↑ 4

A second melodic figure, found in white notes only, is based on two ascending adjacent skips of a perfect fourth.[10] In this figure, an ascending motion is momentarily interrupted by descending stepwise movement. It should be noted that this figure is rarely found inverted.

EXAMPLE 1.28 **ADJACENT SKIPS OF A FOURTH**

[10]Refer to the opening measures of Palestrina's motet: *Exaudi Domine*, page 124.

1.5 TREATMENT OF TEXT

Text Setting   The primary concern in setting a text is with the rhythmic treatment of accented and unaccented syllables. A work, movement, or large subsection should begin on an accented beat with a longer white-note value regardless of the syllabic accent in the initial word. But within a melodic phrase, accented syllables should normally be placed on accented beats and/or be set to longer note values. Also use accented syllables with longer note values to begin melismatic passages. Always consider the length of these phrases and avoid overly long melismas that cannot be sung in a single breath. Rests placed between the phrases of a text should be one to three beats in length for the most part, and should always be initiated on accented beats. After rests between phrases, accented syllables may be placed on any beat, but unaccented syllables should be placed on beats 2 or 4. Repeat individual word phrases as needed, but not single words unless they are separated by punctuation (e.g., Sanctus, Sanctus, Sanctus). In addition to the preceding, observe the following rules when setting a text.

1. All white-note values may carry a syllable except when preceded by a black-note value.

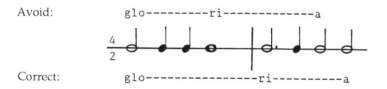

2. At least one white-note value must follow a black-note value before a change in syllables may take place.

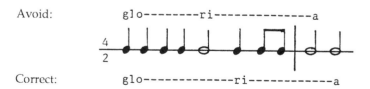

3. Quarter-note passages that begin on a down beat may carry a syllable, but no change may occur during the passage.

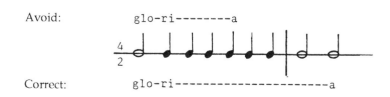

4. Three-syllable words with an accent on the first syllable (Kyrie, Gloria, Spiritu, Domine, Nomine, Sabaoth, etc.) may be set to the ♩. ♩ ♩ rhythmic figure.

Avoid:

Ho----san--na

Correct:

Glo---ri---a

5. Except as noted previously, never change a syllable on an off-beat (either quarter or eighth note).

Avoid:

In   glo---------ri-------a

Correct:

glo------------------------ri--a

6. Repeat a quarter note only on the beat following an anticipation. Except in the anticipation, a repeated note must carry a change of syllable.

7. The text setting must remain the same in imitative passages.

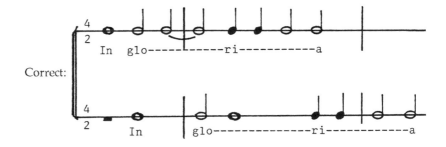

Correct:

In glo-----⌣-----ri----------a

In | glo-------------ri-----------a

8. The final note of a section or movement must carry a syllable provided it is not preceded by a black-note value.

Avoid:

glo--ri-------------a.

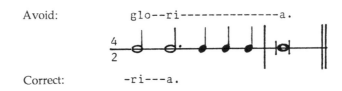

Correct:

-ri---a.

Texts Here are several texts excerpted from the Ordinary which may be used for written exercises. It may be instructive to compare their treatment to various settings found in the musical examples in Appendix I.

1. Ký-ri-e e-lé-i-son (or e-léi-son).   *Lord have mercy,*
    Chrí-ste e-lé-i-son.   *Christ have mercy,*
    Ký-ri-e e-lé-i-son.   *Lord have mercy.*

2(a) Gló-ri-a in ex-cél-sis Dé-o.   *Glory be to God on high.*

  (b) Et in tér-ra pax ho-mí-ni-bus   *And on earth peace to men*
      bó-nae vo-lun-tá-tis.   *of good will.*

  (c) Lau-dá-mus te.   *We praise you.*

  (d) Cum sán-cto Spí-ri-tu,   *With the Holy Ghost,*
      in gló-ri-a Dé-i Pá-tris.   *in the glory of God,*
      Á-men.   *the Father.*
                                              So be it.

3. Crú-ci-fi-xus e-tí-am pro nó-bis,   *He was crucified also for us,*
    sub Pón-ti-o Pi-lá-to pás-sus,   *suffered under Pontius Pilate,*
    et se-púl-tus est.   *and was buried.*

4(a) Sánc-tus, Sánc-tus, Sánc-tus,   *Holy, Holy, Holy,*
     Dó-mi-nus Dé-us Sá-ba-oth.   *Lord God of Hosts.*

  (b) Plé-ni sunt cóe-li et tér-ra   *Heaven and earth are full of*
      gló-ri-a tú-a.   *your glory.*

  (c) Bé-ne-di-ctus qui vé-nit in   *Blessed (is he) who comes in*
      nó-mi-ne Dó-mi-ni.   *the name of the Lord.*

  (d) Ho-sán-na in ex-cél-sis.   *Pray (God) in the highest.*

5(a) Á-gnus Dé-i,   *Lamb of God,*
     qui tól-lis pec-cá-ta mún-di,   *who takes away the sins of*
     mi-se-ré-re nó-bis.   *the world,*
                                              have mercy on us.

  (b) Á-gnus Dé-i,   *Lamb of God,*
      qui tól-lis pec-cá-ta mún-di,   *who takes away the sins of*
      dó-na nó-bis pá-cem.   *the world,*
                                              grant us peace.

2 Counterpoint in Two Parts

2.1 BASIC MATERIALS: WRITING IN TWO PARTS

The development of counterpoint, and its use in multiple-voiced textures, accounts for one of the major differences between Western music and the music of most other cultures. Writings on the theory and practice of counterpoint began to appear as early as the ninth century. By 1725, when Johann Joseph Fux (1660–1741) published his *Gradus ad Parnassum*, the study of species counterpoint and its (free) association with the musical style of Palestrina was well established. Although pedagogical methods based on species counterpoint are not often found today, modern texts on modal or "strict" counterpoint still propose to be based on Palestrina's musical practice. Be that as it may, the study of Renaissance counterpoint continues to be recognized as an integral part of a thorough musical training. In this regard, it is interesting to recall that such composers as Beethoven, Schubert, and Brahms chose to study sixteenth-century counterpoint as a means of further developing and strengthening their compositional craft.

Ideally, contrapuntal composition seeks to combine two or more melodies in a manner that sounds as if no single line has compromised its freedom or individuality for the sake of others. An ideal, remember, is that toward which we strive!

In this style, as in most musical systems, those elements defined as dissonant are restricted in their use and are subject to specific control. Consonant elements, for the most part, are treated freely and may be used in any context at any time.

Harmonic (vertical) intervals are always calculated from the lowest *sounding* note to each successively higher pitch. Compound intervals beyond the ninth or tenth are usually analyzed as the basic interval without its octave component (i.e., an eleventh = a fourth, a thirteenth = a sixth, etc.). Therefore, any restrictions placed on a ⌊2 – 1⌋ suspension apply equally well to a ⌊9 – 8⌋ suspension; restrictions on parallel fifths apply equally well to parallel twelfths, and so on.

The following list of harmonic intervals should not be confused with those intervals listed under melodic skips. For instance, the *harmonic* major sixth may be treated freely as a consonance; but as a *melodic* skip, the major sixth must be avoided. Different functions account for differences in what is allowed.

Harmonic Consonances Perfect unisons, fifths, and octaves
Major and minor thirds and sixths

Harmonic Dissonances Perfect fourths
Major and minor seconds, sevenths and ninths
All augmented and diminished intervals

Voice Movement Two voices may move in any of four ways against each other: contrary, oblique, similar, or parallel.

EXAMPLE 2.1 VOICE MOVEMENT

Parallel movement is limited to thirds and sixths only. Perfect unisons, fifths, and octaves are approached either by oblique or contrary motion. Occasionally, fifths and octaves may be approached in similar motion, but only if one of the voices (preferably the top voice) moves by step.

EXAMPLE 2.2   Voice leading to perfect intervals

When separated by an imperfect consonance, the same perfect interval may occur on alternate beats. Avoid writing more than two different perfect intervals on consecutive beats and always avoid writing parallel perfect intervals.

EXAMPLE 2.3   Treatment of perfect intervals

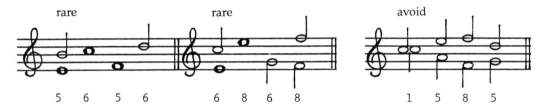

Musica Ficta   As previously mentioned, the accidentals commonly encountered in this style are B♭ and E♭, which are used to correct tritones, and the cadential alterations C♯, F♯, and G♯. Occasionally in Renaissance music, B♭ and E♭ appear to have been used to correct tritone cross relationships between outer voices. Although this practice is not evident in Palestrina's music, surprisingly few cross relationships between outer voices can be found, suggesting that priority was given to their avoidance, rather than to their correction. Carefully compare the progressions in Example 2.5 with those in Example 2.4 and notice how the half-note movement on beat two in Example 2.5 is used to avoid the tritone cross relationship.

EXAMPLE 2.4   Tritone cross relationships

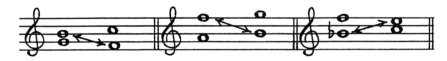

EXAMPLE 2.5   ᴀᴠᴏɪᴅᴀɴᴄᴇ ᴏꜰ ᴛʀɪᴛᴏɴᴇ ᴄʀᴏꜱꜱ ʀᴇʟᴀᴛɪᴏɴꜱʜɪᴘꜱ

Watch for unacceptable intervals created at cadence points by leading tones. Review Example 1.11 on page 8 in this regard.

EXAMPLE 2.6   ᴜɴᴀᴄᴄᴇᴘᴛᴀʙʟᴇ ɪɴᴛᴇʀᴠᴀʟꜱ ᴀᴛ ᴄᴀᴅᴇɴᴄᴇ ᴘᴏɪɴᴛꜱ

Chromaticism should always be avoided and chromatic cross relationships corrected if they occur. Carefully compare the treatment of chromatically altered notes in Example 2.7 with those in Example 2.8.

EXAMPLE 2.7   ᴄʜʀᴏᴍᴀᴛɪᴄᴀʟʟʏ ᴀʟᴛᴇʀᴇᴅ ɴᴏᴛᴇꜱ

(a) Chromaticism

(b) Chromatic cross relationship

(c) Chromaticism and tritone cross relationship

EXAMPLE 2.8   ᴄᴏʀʀᴇᴄᴛ ᴛʀᴇᴀᴛᴍᴇɴᴛ ᴏꜰ ᴛʜᴇꜱᴇ ᴄʜʀᴏᴍᴀᴛɪᴄᴀʟʟʏ ᴀʟᴛᴇʀᴇᴅ ɴᴏᴛᴇꜱ

(a)

(b)

(c)

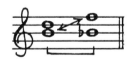

Consonant Writing in Two Parts   When two parts strike simultaneously (or move together in equal note values), they must do so in consonant intervals. (See the only exception, in Example 2.24, page 36.)

EXAMPLE 2.9 **HARMONIC TREATMENT IN TWO PARTS**

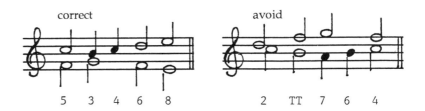

It is suggested that beginning exercises in two parts consist exclusively of consonance, using only breves and whole notes. Study the following guidelines and use Example 2.10 as a model for written work.

1. Begin and end on the final with an octave or unison.

2. Unisons, for the present, should occur only at the beginning and/or at the end; this restriction does not apply to octaves.

3. Enter the final by step in contrary motion with both voices (known as a *clausula vera* cadence).

4. Raise the seventh-scale degree before entering the final in the Aeolian, Dorian, and Mixolydian modes. The penultimate interval will always be either a minor third or a major sixth.

5. Tritone cross relationships need not be corrected. Always correct chromatic cross relationships if they occur; avoid doubling altered notes.

6. Avoid skips in both voices at the same time. The voice opposite a skip should either not move or should move by step.

7. Do not exceed the interval of a tenth between voices. Occasional voice crossing may be used.

8. Limit parallel thirds and sixths to three or four in succession.

9. Observe melodic rules concerning skips and shape and avoid consecutive-note repetitions.

10. Write each part on a separate staff and include an intervallic analysis.

EXAMPLE 2.10 **CONSONANT WRITING IN TWO PARTS USING WHOLE NOTES AND BREVES**

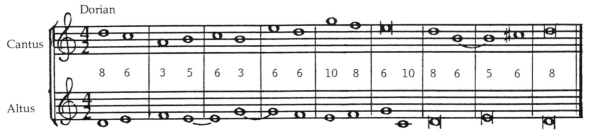

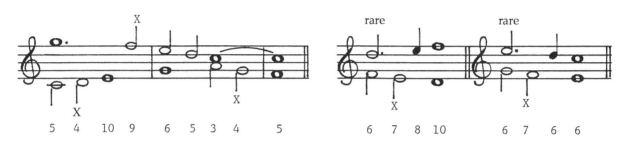

Half-Note Passing Tones

The half-note passing tone is a dissonant half note that is approached by step from above or below and is left by step *in the same direction*. It occurs only on beats 2 or 4 and usually passes against a note at least twice its value.

EXAMPLE 2.11   HALF-NOTE PASSING TONES

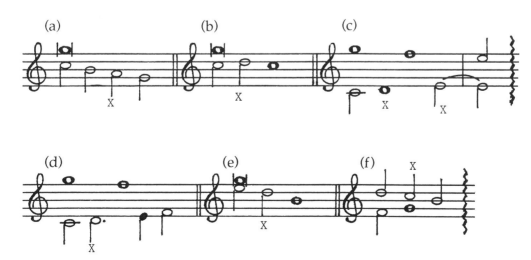

Notice in Example 2.11 that the voice opposite the half-note passing tone may skip. The voice creating a dissonance is referred to as the "dissonating voice"; the opposite voice is referred to as the "nondissonating voice."

Study the following examples for mistakes in the use of the half-note passing tone. *None of the following are acceptable.*

EXAMPLE 2.12   INCORRECT TREATMENT OF THE HALF-NOTE PASSING TONE

Comments on Example 2.12:

(a) The passing tone is on the wrong beat.

(b) A half-note auxiliary is not allowed in $\frac{4}{2}$ meter.

(c) Beat 2 must be a *half* note; in beat 4, never tie a passing tone.

(d) No dotted-note passing tones can be used in this style.

(e) Never skip into or out of a dissonance (see an exception in Example 2.27 on page 38).

(f) Note-against-note dissonance is not allowed (see an exception in Example 2.24 on page 36).

The following example illustrates the use of the half-note passing tone. Notice that for rhythmic balance, each part makes about equal use of the various white-note values. Also, the tritone need not be corrected when treated as a dissonance.

EXAMPLE 2.13   **AN EXERCISE ON THE USE OF HALF-NOTE PASSING TONES**

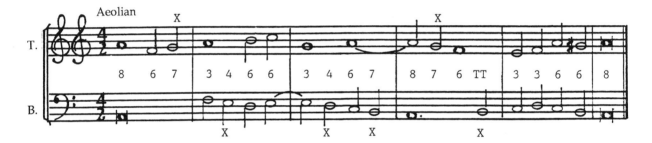

Suspensions   The suspension is the only accented dissonance allowed on beats 1 and 3. All suspensions resolve *downward* by step on the beat following the dissonance (2 or 4). In two parts, the common suspension dissonances are the ⌐7 – 6⌐ and the ⌐2 – 3⌐, although the ⌐4 – 3⌐ suspension may also be used. Notice in the following examples that in the ⌐7 – 6⌐ and ⌐4 – 3⌐ suspensions it is the *upper* voice that is suspended, whereas in the ⌐2 – 3⌐ suspension it is the *lower* voice that is suspended. The opposite (nondissonating) voice may enter the suspension by step or skip. A correctly written suspension requires:

1. A half-note consonant preparation on beats 2 or 4.

2. The half-note suspension dissonance on beats 1 or 3.

3. A half-note downward consonant resolution on beats 2 or 4.

EXAMPLE *2.14*   SUSPENSIONS IN TWO PARTS

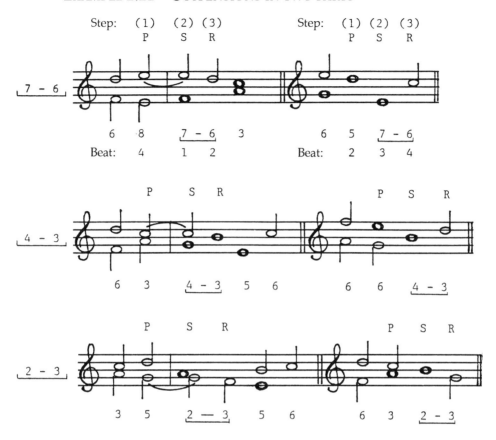

The following examples illustrate some common mistakes in writing suspensions.

EXAMPLE *2.15*   COMMON MISTAKES IN WRITING SUSPENSIONS

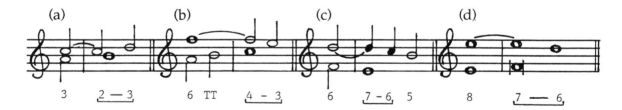

Comments on Example 2.15:

(a) In a 2 – 3 suspension, the lower voice must be suspended and resolved downward by step.

(b) The beat preceding a suspension must always be consonant.

(c) The resolution must occur on beat two, but it may be preceded by an anticipation. (See Example 2.26(c) on page 38.)

(d) A suspension must resolve on beat 2 or 4, although the resolution may be longer in value than a half note.

Final Cadences   Notice in Example 2.16 that, as established in Chapter 1, the seventh scale degree in the Phrygian mode is not raised when used in a cadence. The Phrygian cadence is unique in that the second scale degree (F), being a half step above the final, is considered to be an upper leading tone. Therefore, the seventh scale degree in Phrygian mode was *never* raised (i.e., never use D♯).

EXAMPLE 2.16   THE FINAL CADENCE

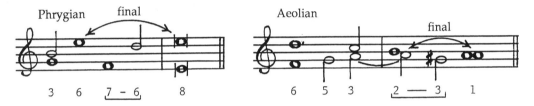

All exercises should now include a ⌊7 – 6⌋ or ⌊2 – 3⌋ suspension on the last accented beat before concluding on the final. Remember that in the concluding cadence, it is the *final* that is always the suspended pitch.

2.2 IMITATION

Writing Imitation   The standard method for beginning a sacred polyphonic composition in the sixteenth century was with imitation. Strict imitation from the beginning of a work to its conclusion is called *canon*.[1] In general practice, composers used strict imitation only in the opening measures, then continued with free composition until reaching an interior cadence, after which new melodic material was again treated in a manner similar to the opening of the work. The practice of beginning a new imitative exposition after each interior cadence was based on the phrase structure of the text and was repeated throughout a complete movement.

Use the following procedure to write imitation:

1. Compose the leading part to the point at which the second part is to commence.

---

[1]Refer to Palestrina's Missa: *O Rex gloriae, Benedictus*, page 104; and to Missa: *Ad fugam, Benedictus*, page 174.

2. Copy the leading part (dux) in the follower (comes), beginning on a primary beat (1 or 3) with the selected pitch for imitation.

3. Compose a counterpart against the follower.

4. Repeat the process (usually 2–4 measures) until free counterpoint is to begin.

EXAMPLE 2.17   WRITING IMITATION

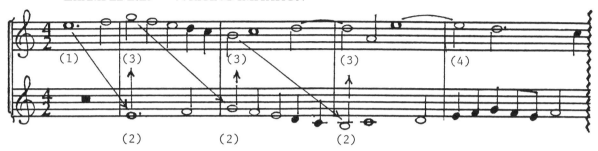

Remember that it is customary to begin with a whole note or a breve; never use a value smaller than a dotted half note.

The follower (comes) in Example 2.17 makes use of a real answer. In a real answer, the intervallic structure of the subject is maintained, except that major and minor intervals are treated as equivalent (i.e., major seconds = minor seconds, etc.).[2] Because the use of imitation was such a common practice, it is not surprising that composers made use of techniques that added some variety to the imitative process. Among these options are those shown in Example 2.18; combining options is also possible, as illustrated in Example 2.18(c).

EXAMPLE 2.18   OTHER FORMS OF IMITATION

(a) Inversion[3]

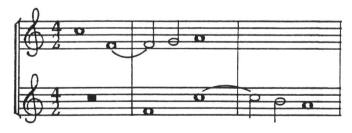

In inversion, reverse the direction of the intervals.

---

[2]An alternate type of answer allows certain intervallic changes in the subject and is called a *tonal answer*. Although tonal answers are more characteristic of later periods, the substitution of a perfect fourth for a fifth (or a fifth for a fourth) may be found in some of Palestrina's imitative answers.

[3]Refer to the opening measures of Palestrina's Magnificat V toni: *Et exsultavit*, page 129 and Motet: *Surrexit pastor bonus*, page 132.

(b) Diminution

In diminution, halve all note values.

(c) Augmentation and Inversion

In augmentation, double all note values.

(d) Retrograde

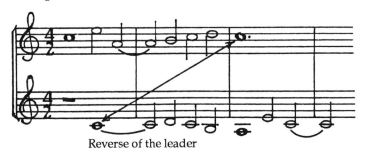

Reverse of the leader

In retrograde, write the subject backwards.

Imitative Entrance Pitches

The choice of initial pitch classes used in the imitative opening of sacred polyphonic compositions might appear to be entirely arbitrary, but basic principles prevail and are rather easy to understand if the three primary modal degrees (the final and dominants of both the authentic and plagal modes) are kept in mind.

In the Mixolydian mode, for example, the various initial pitches used in imitation by Palestrina are:

1. G and G: the final at the octave or unison
2. G and D: the final and dominant

3. G and C: the final and its lower fifth (very common)[4]

4. C and F: the plagal dominant and its lower fifth[5]

5. D, A, and E: the authentic dominant (D), the upper fifth of the dominant (A), and another upper fifth above A (E)[6]

As a generalization, written work may begin with imitation based on the final at the octave (or unison), or on the final and perfect fifth above. The latter is not commonly found in the Phrygian and Aeolian modes, where the final and lower fifth were preferred.

Listed in Example 2.19 are acceptable perfect-fifth associations that may be used as initial pitches in imitation. The leader may use either the upper or lower pitch.

EXAMPLE *2.19*   INITIAL PITCHES IN IMITATION

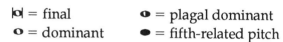

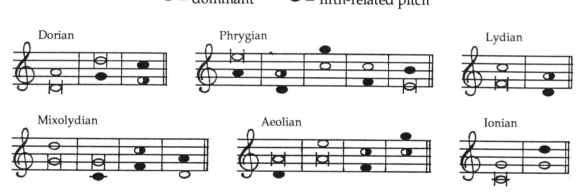

2.3 TREATMENT OF BLACK NOTES

Black-Note Dissonances   In the following discussion, those quarter notes falling on the beat are referred to as "accented"; those falling on the off-beat are referred to as "unaccented." With the single exception of the *nota*

---

[4]When the plagal dominant and the lower fifth of the final are the same pitch, as in the Phrygian and Mixolydian modes, labelling should be based on context, as illustrated by the initial pitches in 3 and 4.

[5]Refer to the opening measures of Palestrina's Hymn: *Lavacra puri*, page 115.

[6]Refer to the opening measures of Palestrina's Missa: *Ad fugam, Benedictus*, page 174.

cambiata, skips to or from dissonant notes are not allowed. Therefore, dissonant quarter and eighth notes must always be stepwise and will either be passing tones, lower auxiliaries, anticipations, or appoggiaturas. Remember, consonant black notes may be treated freely within the melodic constraints discussed in Chapter 1.

Unaccented Quarter- and Eighth-Note Passing Tones

Unaccented quarter-note passing tones may occur on the off-beat of any beat and may ascend or descend. Since eighth-note pairs also occupy this rhythmic placement, they are treated in the same manner.

EXAMPLE 2.20   THE UNACCENTED QUARTER- AND EIGHTH-NOTE PASSING TONE

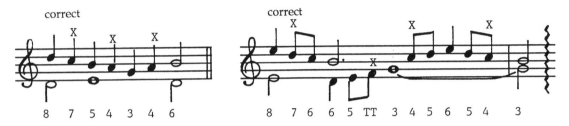

Auxiliary

The auxiliary is similar to the unaccented passing tone in that it may be a quarter- or eighth-note value, it occurs on the off-beat of any beat, and it must always be approached and left by step. The auxiliary, however, always returns to the note that preceded it and normally descends.

Ascending quarter-note auxiliaries are used infrequently and should be avoided; eighth-note configurations of this type are virtually nonexistent.

EXAMPLE 2.21   THE AUXILIARY

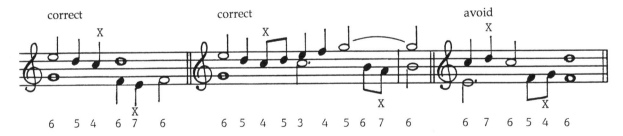

Accented Quarter-Note Passing Tones

The accented quarter-note passing tone is the first of two quarter notes that is approached and left by step in descending motion and occurs on beats 2 or 4 only. Except as noted in Example 2.22, the quarter-note pair is preceded and followed by a white-note value and passes against any value larger than a half note.

EXAMPLE 2.22   THE ACCENTED QUARTER-NOTE PASSING TONE

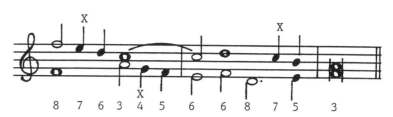

The accented quarter-note passing tone may be preceded by a quarter note if it is a part of a "filled-in" cambiata figure.

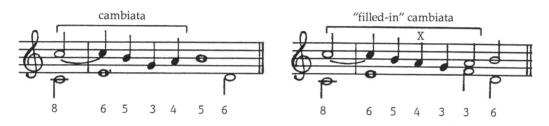

EXAMPLE 2.23   INCORRECT USES OF THE ACCENTED QUARTER-NOTE PASSING TONE

Comments on Example 2.23:

(a) Accented quarter-note passing tones must be descending.

(b) This is not a passing tone; also, auxiliaries only occur on off-beats.

(c) The passing tone is on the wrong beat.

(d) Except as noted in the following discussion, simultaneously struck dissonances should be avoided. Also, the accented quarter-note passing tone must pass against a dotted half note or larger value.

Appoggiatura   As may be seen in Example 2.24, the appoggiatura (APP) shares certain similarities with both the accented quarter-note passing tone (AQPT) and the unaccented eighth-note passing tone (UEPT). Their differences, however, require special attention.

1. The appoggiatura dissonance is struck *simultaneously* with the opposite voice, resulting in the only exception to such restrictions commonly found in the style.

2. The appoggiatura is always approached and left by step in descending motion and occurs on beats 2 or 4 as two quarter notes against a whole note or on the off-beats of 2 or 4 as two eighth notes against a quarter note.

3. The voice opposite the appoggiatura may approach the dissonance in oblique motion, by step or skip in contrary motion, or (rarely) by step in similar motion.

4. Although the appoggiatura frequently occurs in, or directly before, a suspension, its use is not restricted in this regard.

EXAMPLE 2.24   THE APPOGGIATURA

Compare the following:

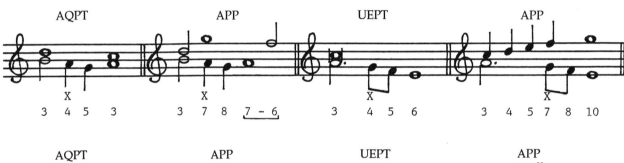

A consecutive dissonance will result if the appoggiatura is approached in contrary direction from an unaccented quarter-note passing tone, and a parallel dissonance if approached from an unaccented quarter-note passing tone in similar motion. It should be noted that the use of any type of consecutive dissonance is quite rare in this style.

The following examples are drawn from the music of Palestrina.

2.4 HARMONIC TREATMENT OF MELODIC IDIOMS

Anticipation
(*Portamento*)

The anticipation occurs as a quarter-note value that descends by step on the off-beat of 1 or 3. (Refer to Example 1.25, page 16.) It may be consonant or dissonant, but the note following the anticipation must be consonant. Anticipations that ascend are rarely used and should be avoided.

EXAMPLE 2.25   T̄HE ANTICIPATION

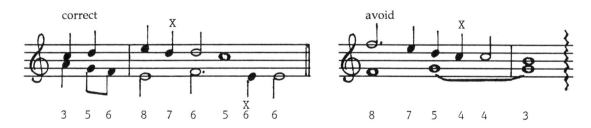

Suspension Ornamentations

As shown in Example 2.26, the anticipation and auxiliary frequently serve as melodic ornamentation in the resolution of suspensions. Illustrations (a) and (b) are commonly found in final cadences, but illustrations (c) and (d) should be avoided in that context. In illustration (e), ornamental dissonances are used to embellish the beats preceding and following the suspension in the upper voice.

EXAMPLE 2.26 SUSPENSION ORNAMENTATIONS

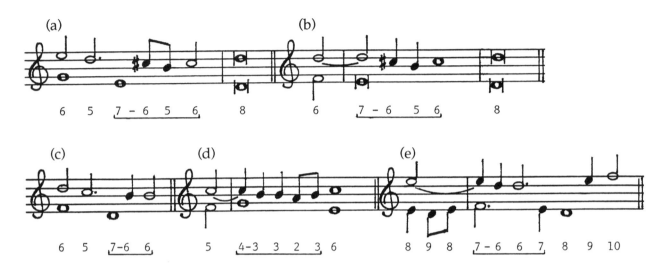

Nota Cambiata

The cambiata figure includes the only exception to the restriction on a skip from a dissonance commonly found in the style. In the cambiata figure, the initial dotted half note *must remain consonant*; the second note may be consonant or dissonant; the third note must be consonant, and the fourth note may be either a dissonant passing tone or a consonance, depending on its rhythmic placement.

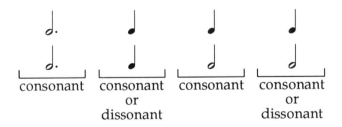

EXAMPLE 2.27 THE *NOTA CAMBIATA*: HARMONIC TREATMENT

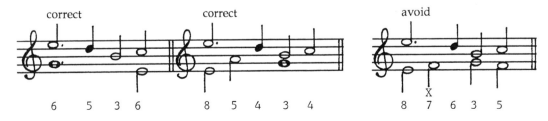

Placement of Dissonances: A Summary

On beats 1 and 3:	Suspension

On the off-beats of 1 and 3:
Anticipation (↓ only)
Cambiata escape tone
Lower auxiliary
Unaccented quarter-note passing tone (↑ and ↓)

On beats 2 and 4:
Half-note passing tone (↑ and ↓)
Accented quarter-note passing tone (↓ only)
Appoggiatura (as ♩♩ against o, ↓ only)

On the off-beats of 2 and 4:
Appoggiatura (as ♫ against ♩, ↓ only)
Cambiata escape tone
Lower auxiliary
Unaccented quarter-note passing tone (↑ and ↓)

Interior Cadences

Interior cadences are used to demarcate subsections in a musical work and to help delineate and clarify the phrase structure of the text. When used for textual purposes, interior cadences allow for a brief reduction in the total number of voices without interrupting the rhythmic and sonic flow of the music. Although a text is not included in Example 2.28, it serves to illustrate the latter, nonconclusive, type of interior cadence.[7]

In the first of the two examples, both voices resolve to a cadence point; the bottom voice then drops out to begin a new imitative subject, while the top voice continues to sound. In the second example, often called a *hocket* cadence, the voice carrying the leading tone goes to the cadence point, but the second voice drops out before doing so.

EXAMPLE 2.28   INTERIOR CADENCES

(a) Mixolydian

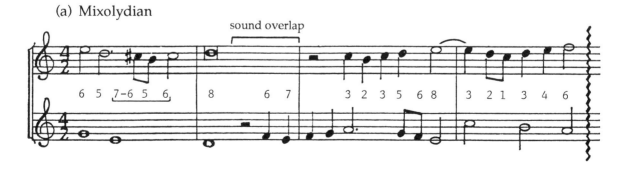

----

[7]See Lassus' *Sancti mei*, measures 12 and 17, page 89.

(b) Dorian

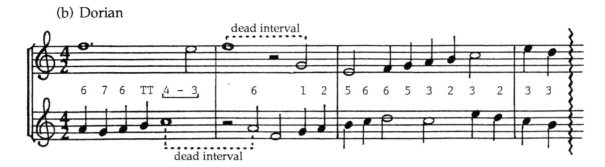

When writing interior cadences, observe the following:

1. Use new imitative material following an interior cadence; however, any rhythmic value may be used to initiate that imitation.

2. Rests in interior cadences are usually limited to whole and/or half values and occur only on accented beats. Note that interior points of imitation normally begin on beats 2 or 4.

3. Any pitch may follow the rest, regardless of the melodic interval created with the previous pitch (known as a "dead interval").

4. Remember that in the *hocket* cadence, the voice carrying the leading tone must go to the cadence point.

Interior Cadence Points

To choose cadence points for interior cadences, use the same process as was used for choosing imitative entrance pitches. (Refer to Example 2.19, page 33.) Show a preference for the primary modal degrees, although using the upper and lower fifths of these degrees is acceptable and provides greater variety. However, observe the following reservations:[8]

1. Never cadence on pitch class B.

2. Cadence on pitch class E (the lower fifth of B) only in the Phrygian mode.

3. Cadence on pitch class F (the upper [diminished] fifth of B) only in the Lydian and Dorian modes.

One final word on coordinating entrance pitches with interior cadence points. When the final and/or dominant are used as imitative entrance pitches, secondary pitch classes (upper and lower fifths) may freely be used as interior cadence points. Reverse this

---

[8]In Ionian mode, for example, cadence points would be C (final), G (dominant), A (lower fifth of the plagal dominant), and D (the upper fifth of the dominant). The plagal dominant, E, with its upper fifth, B, would not be used. The lower fifth of the final, F, would also be eliminated. Therefore, cadence on C, G, A, or D.

process if the entrance pitches include secondary pitch classes. For example, in a work in Dorian mode in which F and C (the plagal dominant and its upper fifth) are used as imitative entrance pitches, use D and/or A for interior cadences in order to bring the mode into focus. Interior cadences on F and C would suggest Lydian mode and would be confusing tonally. In actual practice, this lack of modal focus caused a virtual merging of various modes (Aeolian and Phrygian, for instance) and probably contributed significantly to the breakdown of the modal system. Finally, imitation after interior cadences in two-part works may be based on any interval except the tritone.[9]

The two illustrations of Example 2.29 are schematic reductions of Hymn: *In Festo Transfigurationis Domini* by Palestrina and *Oculus non vidit* by Lassus that illustrate initial imitative pitches and cadences. While stylistic similarity is obvious, the variety of intervals used for imitation (the unison, octave, fifth, and seventh) by Lassus is in sharp contrast to Palestrina's preference for perfect fifths. The work by Palestrina is orderly, structurally balanced, and of a restrained elegance. The Lassus example illustrates the kind of absorbing, richly inventive music that can result from a probing, exploratory mind.

EXAMPLE 2.29   INITIAL IMITATIVE PITCHES AND CADENCES

Measure numbers are shown above the staff and pitch identification below.

Key to Symbols

F = Final
D = Dominant
PD = Plagal dominant
L = Lower fifth of the . . .
U = Upper fifth of the . . .
● = Initial pitch of imitation
o = Cadence pitch

(a) Phrygian

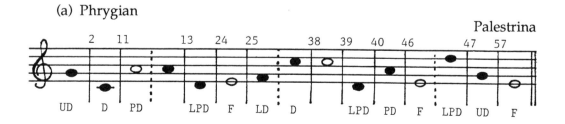

_____

[9]The interval of imitation is of considerably less importance than the fact that some rational basis be used in selecting those particular pitches.

(b) Dorian

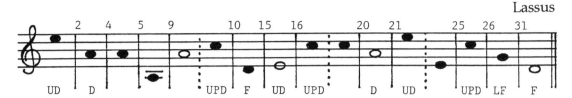

Unisons   In addition to the imitative opening and cadential close of an exercise, unisons may occur in interior cadences after a ⌊2 – 3⌋ suspension, as internal imitative beginnings, and freely as black-note values.

In the last situation, unisons are approached in contrary or oblique motion by step or skip. However, the restrictions on parallel perfect intervals still remain. Example 2.30 illustrates typical usage found in both Lassus and Palestrina.

EXAMPLE 2.30   UNISONS IN BLACK-NOTE VALUES

Unisons on the beat

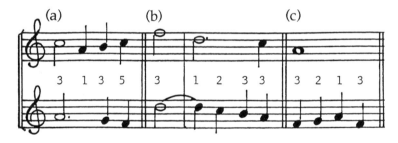

Unisons on the off-beat

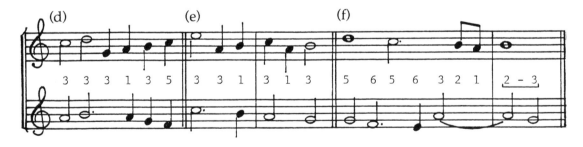

Rhythm in Counterpoint   Because of the homogeneity of tone color in choral groups, rhythm becomes the most important factor in maintaining melodic autonomy. When a rhythmic scheme is doubled by two or more voices, the contrapuntal independence of the lines tend to fuse into a chordal, harmonic block of sound. The descriptive term "familiar style" is often applied to those sections in which polyphony gives way to homophony in this manner. Such contrasting sections were used primarily for textual clarity.

When writing counterpoint, it is important that the voices maintain a considerable amount of rhythmic dissimilarity. Therefore, avoid using homorhythmic values for more than a measure at a time, and balance longer note values in one part with shorter values in the opposite part.

Often, it is helpful to reduce parts to their respective rhythmic schemes, as shown in Example 2.31. Study these schematic reductions from Lassus' *Cantiones duarum vocum.*[10] Notice that in Example 2.31(a) and (b) there appears to be a studied avoidance of simultaneous articulations, whereas Example 2.31(c) illustrates a more balanced stylistic norm. This type of writing not only enhances contrapuntal independence, but promotes textual understanding by limiting syllabic clashes between the voices.

Similar analyses of a variety of works by Palestrina reveal that there is an average of two simultaneous articulations per measure and that these incidents tend to decrease as the number of parts increase. In the two-part works by Lassus the average remains about the same, although the average shows a significant increase in proportion to quarter-note activity.

EXAMPLE *2.31* RHYTHMIC REDUCTION

(a)

(b)

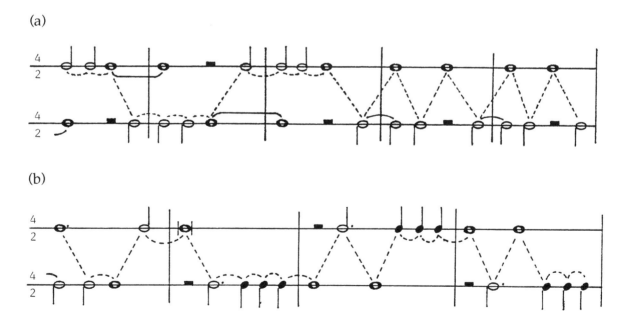

[10]Refer to Lassus' *Serve bone,* measures 19–23, page 92, for Part (a), and measures 1–6, page 91, for Part (c). Part (b) is drawn from *Justi tulerunt,* measures 26–29, page 88.

(c)

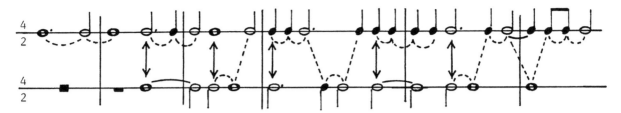

2.5 INVERTIBLE COUNTERPOINT

Invertible (Double) Counterpoint

When counterpoint is written so that any of its parts can serve as a bass to the others, it is referred to as **invertible counterpoint**. If invertible counterpoint is written for two parts, it is called **double counterpoint**; if written for three parts, **triple counterpoint**, and so on. Do not be confused by the term "invertible" when used in this context. The process of inversion, in this case, deals with intervallic inversion, not melodic inversion, and its purpose is to assure that contrapuntal lines be interchangeable; that is, to make it possible to shuffle the parts like a deck of cards. In practice, invertible counterpoint is usually found in sections of two to four measures that return inverted (i.e., with the parts rearranged) within the same number of measures.[11]

In writing double counterpoint, it is necessary to know what the resulting intervals between the two voices will be when they are rearranged. The following table gives the complementary intervals for invertible counterpoint at the octave:

The original interval: 1 2 3 4 5 6 7 8
The inversion yields: 8 7 6 5 4 3 2 1

The table shows that since octaves convert to unisons, they must occur as black-note values and that fifths must be treated as dissonances because they convert to fourths.

The following example gives a double analysis of both the original interval and the interval of inversion. Such an analysis will prove helpful in anticipating and avoiding the incorrect treatment of dissonances.

---

[11]An example of invertible counterpoint at the octave may be found in Palestrina's Missa: *Ave Maria, Pleni sunt coeli* on page 106. Compare measures 12–14 with measures 17–19.

EXAMPLE 2.32   **DOUBLE COUNTERPOINT AT THE OCTAVE**

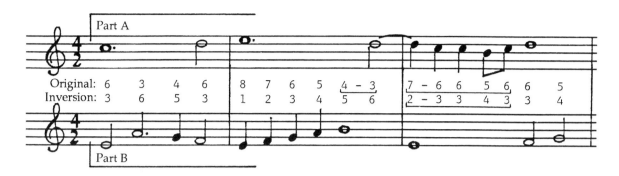

Notice in Example 2.32 that the ⌐4 – 3⌐ suspension in measure 2 is lost when inverted, but that the ⌐7 – 6⌐ suspension returns as a ⌐2 – 3⌐ suspension. Finally, the last half note in Part B must be treated as a half-note passing tone in the inversion.

Example 2.33 shows Parts A and B inverted. Part B remains at its original pitch level, whereas Part A appears one octave lower (this process could be reversed, of course).

EXAMPLE 2.33   **EXCHANGE OF PARTS**

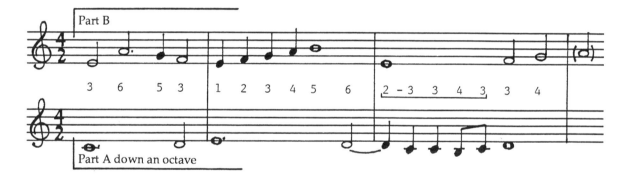

If this example were intended for two sopranos, it could not be used because the lower part exceeds the soprano's lower range. If Part A remained at its pitch level and Part B were transposed up an octave, it would exceed the upper vocal range. Therefore, for reasons of vocal range, it is necessary to transpose Part A down less than an octave, and to transpose Part B up the remainder of the octave. For example, by transposing Part A down a fifth, Part B would need to be transposed up a fourth. To determine these complementary up-and-down transpositions, simply refer to the original table for invertible counterpoint at the octave. Let the top line represent the downward transposition and the lower line the upward interval of transposition:

Interval down (↓): 1 2 3 4 5 etc.
Interval up   (↑): 8 7 6 5 4 etc.

It is important to remember that the unison is designated as number one (1), and indicates that no transposition is to be made.

The following graph illustrates how Example 2.32 is used in a short exercise.

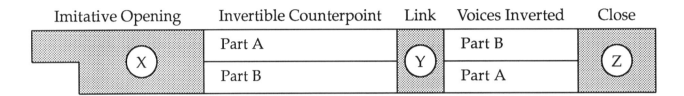

An imitative opening (Section X) was written to connect to the prewritten invertible counterpoint. Next, a short link (Section Y) was needed to secure a smooth transition to the voice inversion. To conclude, a suitable close (Section Z) was added to end on the final.

EXAMPLE 2.34   AN EXERCISE USING INVERTIBLE COUNTERPOINT

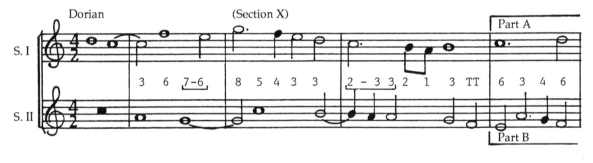

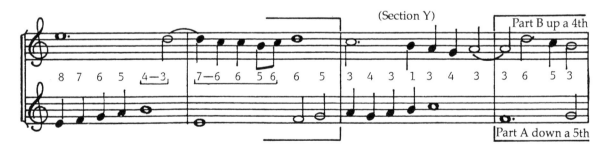

Invertible Counterpoint at the Tenth

All parallel movement is effectively eliminated in invertible counterpoint at the tenth because thirds invert to octaves and sixths to fifths. Additionally, the ⌊2 – 3⌋ suspension is the only suspension possible in this combination.

Table for Invertible Counterpoint at the Tenth

1	2	3	4	5	6	7	8	9	10
10	9	8	7	6	5	4	3	2	1

Invertible Counterpoint at the Twelfth

Invertible counterpoint at the twelfth is one of the most frequently encountered forms.[12] The only problematic interval is the sixth, which inverts to the seventh. All suspensions are possible, but in the ⌊7 – 6⌋ suspension the sixth must be treated as a half-note passing tone and must be continued downward by step.

Table for Invertible Counterpoint at the Twelfth

1	2	3	4	5	6	7	8	9	10	11	12
12	11	10	9	8	7	6	5	4	3	2	1

Invertible Counterpoint at the Fifteenth

Double counterpoint at the fifteenth (two octaves) has exactly the same inversional properties as that at the octave. Its advantage over double counterpoint at the octave is that compound intervals (up to the fifteenth) may be used between the voices, allowing greater freedom in melodic writing.

Table for Invertible Counterpoint at the Fifteenth

1	2	3	4	5	6	7	8	9	10	11	12	13	14	15
15	14	13	12	11	10	9	8	7	6	5	4	3	2	1

The following suggestions will prove helpful when writing invertible counterpoint.

1. Carefully review the intervallic tables for problem intervals and the inversional results of suspensions.

2. Avoid allowing the distance between the voices to exceed the interval of invertible counterpoint. Doing so voids the inherent variety of complementary intervals (e. g., a tenth between voices in double counterpoint at the octave yields a third, rather than a sixth, when inverted).

3. To help integrate sections of invertible counterpoint in a more musically convincing way, write the initial section of invert-

---

[12]A short example of invertible counterpoint at the twelfth may be found in Lassus' *Sancti mei*, measures 1–3 and 4–6, page 89.

ible counterpoint in your exercise at the point where you wish it to occur. Not only will this enable your writing to unfold in a continuous, forward manner, but the use of a double analysis in this section will reveal any incorrect use of dissonance that may later occur in the inversion. This method will also prove to be of considerable help when setting a text.

Text Setting

Refer to the discussion of text setting in Chapter 1, pages 19–20. Remember that with regard to text setting and the use of final syllables, interior cadences must be treated like final cadences.

Rests and Text Setting

In place of interior cadences, rests were frequently used to separate various phrases of the text. They usually occur on beats 1 or 3, are a whole and/or half value, and are often followed by new imitative material. Refer to the discussion under *Interior Cadences*, pages 39–40, for the characteristics of interior points of imitation.

Suggested Exercise Format with Text

Continue to place your analysis between the upper and lower parts. Place the text above the upper part and below the lower part.

EXAMPLE 2.35   **AN EXERCISE FORMAT IN DORIAN**

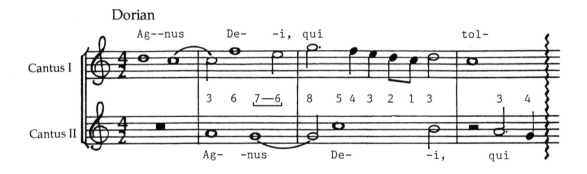

3 Counterpoint in Three Parts

3.1 BASIC MATERIALS: WRITING IN THREE PARTS

The triad serves as the basic harmonic unit in modal counterpoint in three or more parts. All parts are calculated from the lowest *sounding* pitch, which, due to the crossing of parts, may or may not be in the lowest voice part. Without doublings, consonant notes above the lowest pitch will yield major or minor triads in root position $\left(\begin{smallmatrix}5\\3\end{smallmatrix}\right)$ and first inversion $\left(\begin{smallmatrix}6\\3\end{smallmatrix}\right)$. All consonant combinations above the bass note may be used (for example, $\begin{smallmatrix}8\\5\end{smallmatrix}$, $\begin{smallmatrix}6\\6\end{smallmatrix}$, $\begin{smallmatrix}5\\1\end{smallmatrix}$, etc.) *except* for the $\begin{smallmatrix}6\\5\end{smallmatrix}$ combination. Diminished triads must be used in first inversion to avoid the tritone between the root and fifth, as must augmented triads to avoid the augmented fifth between its root and fifth.

EXAMPLE 3.1   THE USE OF AUGMENTED AND DIMINISHED TRIADS

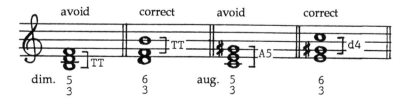

Augmented triads rarely occur, but diminished triads exist diatonically in every mode as a root-position triad on pitch class B and may also result from the use of accidentals to create leading tones in cadences.

Voice Movement

Example 3.1 suggests that harmonic events between upper voices are of no consequence. Although a considerable amount of dissonance may be found at times, it is always necessary to consider the harmonic interaction between upper voices when writing in three (or more) parts.

While tritones and parallel fourths may now occur between upper voices, the restriction on parallel unisons, octaves, and fifths remains. As shown in Example 3.2, parallel fifths may not be revealed through analysis. Upper-voice movement must always be checked for unacceptable parallels and voice leading.

EXAMPLE 3.2   VOICE LEADING BETWEEN UPPER PARTS

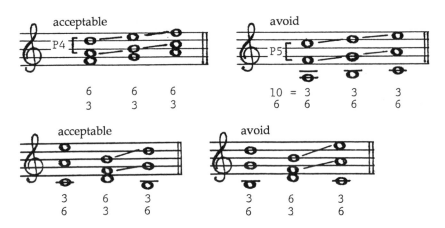

Musica Ficta

No additional *musica ficta* is allowed in multiple-voice counterpoint and its use must remain functional. Also, do not double altered modal degrees, cadential alterations, or diatonic scale degrees when used functionally in cadences (i. e., D and F in Phrygian, B in Ionian, and E in Lydian). The B diminished triad may be converted to a major triad by using B♭, but F♯ should not be used to correct harmonic or melodic tritones.

Consonant Writing in Three Parts

As in two-part writing, beginning exercises in three parts will consist of consonances only, and will use breves and whole notes.[1]

---

[1]Refer to Palestrina's Lamentation: *Feria VI, Lectio II, Filii Sion*, page 93, and Lamentation: *Feria VI, Lectio III, Vetustam fecit*, page 166, as examples based on this approach to writing in three parts.

Four cadential configurations without suspensions are possible. Notice that the first three illustrations in Example 3.3 include the *clausula vera* cadence.

EXAMPLE 3.3   CADENCES WITHOUT SUSPENSIONS

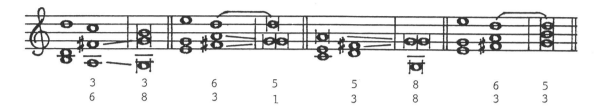

The following points will be helpful in writing beginning exercises in three parts. The musical examples provide a format on which to base written work.

1. Begin on the final in all voices. The concluding sonority may consist of a complete triad, the final and upper fifth (or third), or the final only. Concluding triads must be major and the final must always be present in the lowest sounding voice.

2. Unisons may occur between any two voices, and any chord member may be doubled, except for leading tones in cadences. However, strive to maintain full triadic sonority.

3. Generally, keep adjacent voice parts within a tenth of each other.

4. Use *musica ficta* to create major chords in final cadences, for leading-tone purposes, and to correct tritones and chromatic cross relationships.

5. Avoid simultaneous skips in all voices and consecutive-note repetitions.

6. Limit parallel $^6_3$ chords to 3 or 4 in succession.

7. Observe melodic rules concerning skips and shape.

8. Always write each part on a separate staff.

9. Always include an intervallic analysis. Remember that the analysis is made successively from the lowest sounding voice to each of the upper voices. Due to voice crossing, additional analytical information may be required, as shown in measure 1 of Example 3.4.

EXAMPLE 3.4 CONSONANT WRITING IN THREE PARTS USING WHOLE NOTES AND BREVES

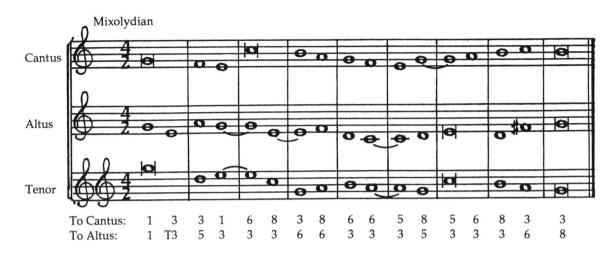

| To Cantus: | 1 | 3 | 3 | 1 | 6 | 8 | 3 | 8 | 6 | 6 | 5 | 8 | 5 | 6 | 8 | 3 | 3 |
| To Altus: | 1 | T3 | 5 | 3 | 3 | 3 | 6 | 6 | 3 | 3 | 3 | 5 | 3 | 3 | 3 | 6 | 8 |

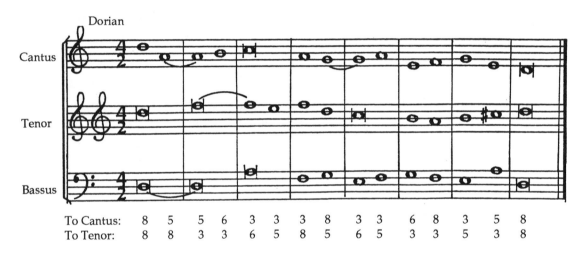

| To Cantus: | 8 | 5 | 5 | 6 | 3 | 3 | 3 | 8 | 3 | 3 | 6 | 8 | 3 | 5 | 8 |
| To Tenor: | 8 | 8 | 3 | 3 | 6 | 5 | 8 | 5 | 6 | 5 | 3 | 3 | 5 | 3 | 8 |

3.2 WHITE-NOTE DISSONANCES AND SUSPENSIONS

Half-Note Passing Tones

Previous restrictions on the placement and treatment of the half-note passing tone remain. Add the following when writing in three or more parts, as explained and illustrated in Example 3.5.

(a) A half-note passing tone may be dissonant against one or more parts.

(b) Doubled half-note passing tones in contrary motion must be unisons, octaves, thirds, or sixths.

(c) Doubled half-note passing tones in parallel motion must be thirds or sixths.

(d) Skips against half-note passing tones must be consonant with both voices.

(e) When a fifth and a sixth simultaneously occur above the bass, one of the intervals must be treated as a passing tone.

EXAMPLE 3.5   THE HALF-NOTE PASSING TONE IN THREE PARTS

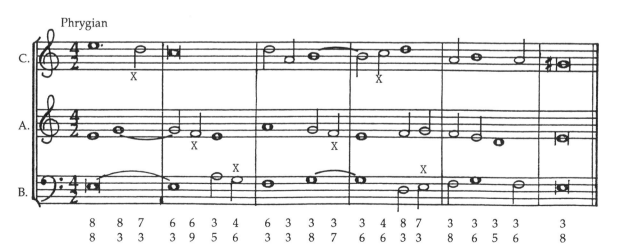

Example 3.6 illustrates the use of the half-note passing tone in a three-part texture. Remember to distribute rhythmic values equally among parts for balance and musical interest.

EXAMPLE 3.6   AN EXERCISE USING HALF-NOTE PASSING TONES

Suspensions   Suspensions in three parts are treated like those in two parts. In upper-voice suspensions, the third voice must be consonant with the bass, but using the note of resolution with the suspended dissonance $\left(\text{e. g., } \frac{\lfloor 4 - 3 \rfloor}{3}\right)$ should be avoided.

The $\lfloor 4 - 3 \rfloor$ suspension is one of the most frequently used in multiple-voice works, its use being preferred in final cadences as well. The three common $\lfloor 4 - 3 \rfloor$ suspensions are $\frac{5}{4}$, $\frac{6}{4}$, and $\frac{8}{4}$.

EXAMPLE 3.7   THE $\lfloor \mathbf{4 - 3} \rfloor$ SUSPENSION

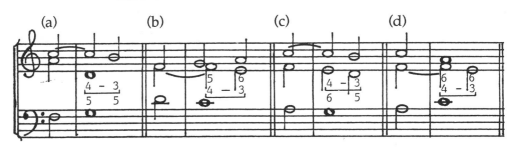

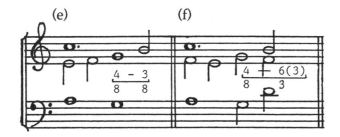

The use of the tritone as a suspension dissonance $\lfloor TT - 3 \rfloor$ occurs infrequently, but may be found, and is treated as is any other $\lfloor 4 - 3 \rfloor$ suspension. When pitch class B occurs in the base, the $\frac{5}{4}$ combination results in a tritone above the bass and must be avoided.

EXAMPLE 3.8   THE TRITONE IN THE $\lfloor \mathbf{4 - 3} \rfloor$ SUSPENSION

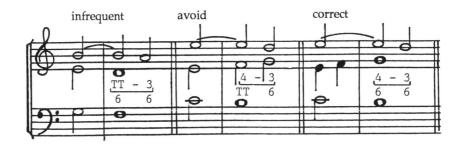

The intervals that may be added to the $\lfloor 7 - 6 \rfloor$ suspension are the third $\binom{7}{3}$, the fifth $\binom{7}{5}$, or the octave $\binom{8}{7}$. The sixth $\binom{7}{6}$ must be excluded because the note of resolution is included with the suspension dissonance. The addition of the third, which is the most common interval, results in a $\frac{6}{3}$ resolution. If the fifth is used, a $\frac{6}{5}$ dissonant combination results, requiring the fifth to move to another pitch on the beat of resolution.

EXAMPLE 3.9   THE $\lfloor 7 - 6 \rfloor$ SUSPENSION

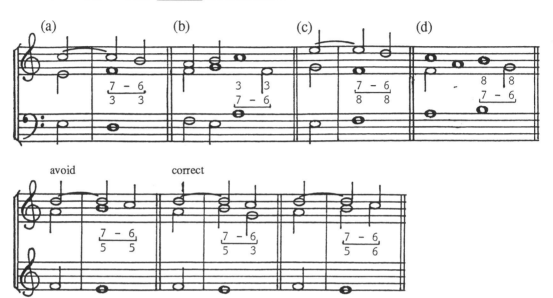

It is possible for the nondissonating voices to step or skip from the suspension dissonance, providing that the voice movement results in consonant combinations. However, the dissonating voice (suspension voice) must always resolve down by step. Study the alternate resolutions of the $\lfloor 7 - 6 \rfloor$ suspension provided in illustrations (a)–(d) of Example 3.10.

EXAMPLE 3.10   ALTERNATE RESOLUTIONS OF THE $\lfloor 7 - 6 \rfloor$ SUSPENSION

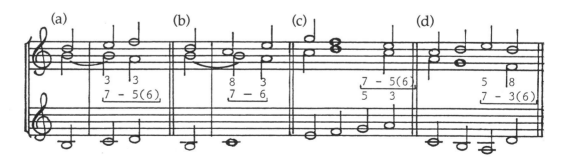

Although the 4 – 5 and 7 – 8 combinations appear in the ₍2 – 3₎ suspension, they should not be thought of as forming double suspensions because, as may be recalled, the 4 – 5 and 7 – 8 never appear alone as suspensions. Although the 4 – 5 occurs frequently in the ₍2 – 3₎ suspension, the 7 – 8 is generally avoided. On occasion, the ₍2 – 3₎ suspension may be found doubled $\left(\begin{smallmatrix} 9-10 \\ 2-3 \end{smallmatrix}\right)$. The three common ₍2 – 3₎ suspensions are $\frac{4}{2}$, $\frac{5}{2}$, and $\frac{6}{2}$. The $\frac{6}{2}$ suspension will result in a $\frac{7}{3}$ resolution and therefore requires that the voice carrying the sixth move to a note consonant with the bass.

EXAMPLE 3.11   THE ₍2 – 3₎ SUSPENSION

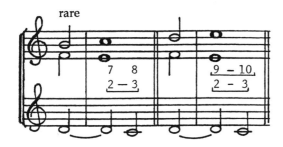

The ₍9 – 8₎ and ₍2 – 1₎ suspensions occur in the $\frac{9-8}{3-3}$ and $\frac{3-3}{2-1}$ configurations. Although the ₍2 – 1₎ suspension was rarely used, the ₍9 – 8₎ suspension occurs with considerable frequency. As shown in Example 3.12, the ₍9 – 8₎ suspension often precedes a ₍4 – 3₎ suspension.

EXAMPLE 3.12   THE ₍9 – 8₎ AND ₍2 – 1₎ SUSPENSIONS

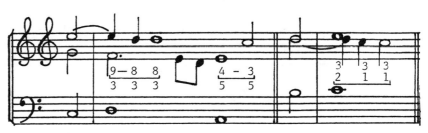

Double Suspensions   The $\lfloor 4 - 3 \rfloor$ suspension serves as the basis for two double suspensions found in three (or more) parts: $\frac{7}{4} - \frac{6}{3}$ and $\frac{9}{4} - \frac{8}{3}$. If the $\lfloor 4 - 3 \rfloor$ occurs over the $\lfloor 7 - 6 \rfloor$, $\left(\frac{4-3}{7-6} \right)$, parallel fifths result on resolution and require the use of ornamentation in one of the upper parts.[2]

EXAMPLE 3.13   DOUBLE SUSPENSIONS

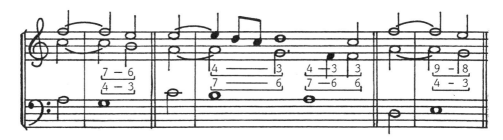

3.3 CADENCES

Conclusive Cadences   As in two parts, conclusive cadences in three parts require that the final be the suspended pitch. With the exception of works in the Phrygian mode, the $\lfloor 4 - 3 \rfloor$ suspension was preferred for conclusive cadences.[3] In the $\lfloor 4 - 3 \rfloor$ conclusive cadence, the bass must skip up a fourth or down a fifth to the final; the leading tone must resolve up a step, but the third voice may go to the final, third (major), or fifth, depending on suitable voice leading. The $\frac{5}{4}$ combination was preferred to the $\frac{6}{4}$ or $\frac{8}{4}$ in final cadences.

EXAMPLE 3.14   CONCLUSIVE CADENCES USING THE $\lfloor 4 - 3 \rfloor$ SUSPENSION

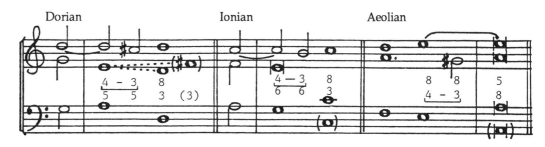

---

[2]An example of the $\frac{9-8}{4-3}$ suspension may be found in Palestrina's Magnificat IV toni: *Fecit potentiam*, measure 16, page 110, and the $\frac{7-6}{4-3}$ suspension in Motet: *Exaudi Domine*, measure 67, page 129, and in Lamentation: *Feria VI, Lectio III, Beth*, measure 85, page 165.

[3]Works in the Phrygian mode usually conclude with either a $\lfloor 7 - 6 \rfloor$ conclusive cadence or a plagal cadence. (See Example 3.16 and illustration (b) of Example 3.17.)

EXAMPLE 3.15   CONCLUSIVE CADENCES USING THE ⌊7 – 6⌋ SUSPENSION

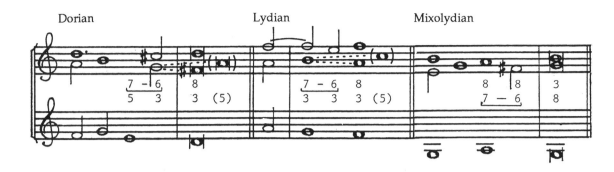

The Phrygian cadence, with its characteristic upper leading tone (F♮), makes exclusive use of the ⌊7 – 6⌋ suspension. (The ⌊4 – 3⌋ is unsuitable for a number of reasons.) A transposed version of the Phrygian cadence is frequently found in the Aeolian mode, resulting in a $\begin{smallmatrix} B^\flat \\ G^\natural \end{smallmatrix} \!\!>\! A$ resolution.

EXAMPLE 3.16   THE PHRYGIAN CADENCE

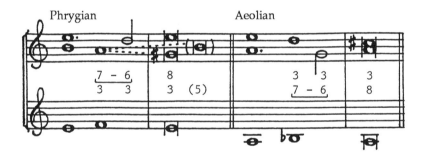

The cadence type, now referred to as "plagal," occurs as a conclusive cadence with considerable frequency in Palestrina's music. A chord based on the lower fifth of the final precedes the final chord to which it resolves (i. e., IV – I); this penultimate "IV" chord may or may not be preceded by a suspension. In illustration (a) of Example 3.17, B♭ is used as a Phrygian inflection (upper leading tone) to the fifth of the final chord.[4] This practice is related to the transposed Phrygian cadence on pitch class A, shown in Example 3.16.

---

[4]The melodic sequence A–B♭–A, frequently used in modes other than Dorian, occurs in transposed Dorian as D–E♭–D. See Palestrina's Lamentation: *Feria VI, Lectio II, Filii Sion*, Tenor I, measure 7, page 93, and Baritone, measures 14 and 19, page 94.

EXAMPLE 3.17 CONCLUSIVE "PLAGAL" CADENCES

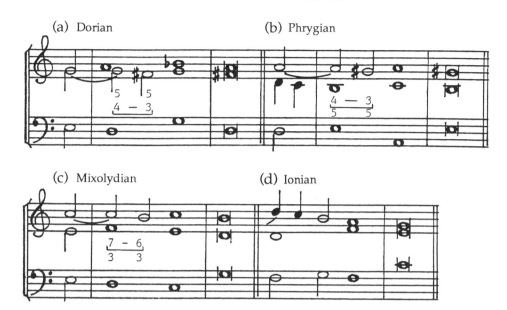

Interior Cadences

As in two parts, interior cadences should make use of imitative overlap to avoid a sonic break in the texture (refer to Example 2.28 on pages 39–40). Although these cadences are usually based on a ⌊4 – 3⌋ or ⌊7 – 6⌋ conclusive cadential pattern, they may resolve to an unexpected chord to create a "deceptive" cadence (Example 3.16(b)). In either case, the first voice to drop out begins a new imitative sequence while at least one of the remaining voices continues to sound (Example 3.18(a)).

EXAMPLE 3.18 **(a) INTERIOR CADENCE**
(b) ALTERNATE RESOLUTIONS FOR USE IN INTERIOR CADENCES

Interior Cadence Points

Refer to Example 2.19 and to the discussion of *Interior Cadence Points* in Chapter 2, pages 40–41.

3.4 IMITATION

To write imitation in three parts, use the same procedure established for writing in two parts. Imitative entrances may be equally or unequally spaced, but do not overly delay the third voice entrance. In addition to the different types of imitation illustrated in Example 2.18 on page 31, it is possible to use imitation between any two voices, allowing the third melodic freedom.

Imitative Entrance Pitches

Fifth-related pitches for imitation are a pervasive characteristic of Palestrina's style. After interior cadences, imitation at the third may be found, but even here, fifth-related entrances are given preference. Imitative answers are usually real and, in four or more parts, voices are frequently paired through the use of different subjects.[5]

Although the fifth relationship is a stylistic norm, different methods for choosing these pitches were apparently used. The first (and most common) method uses the final, or one of the dominants, plus an upper or lower fifth. In the case of the Phrygian and Aeolian modes, the final and lower fifth were given preference.[6] Works in three parts may use these pitches in any order. For instance, using the final (E) and lower fifth (A) in the Phrygian mode, entrance pitches might occur as EAE, EEA, AEA or AAE.

A second method uses ascending or descending fifths to arrive at a primary modal degree which results in three (or more) different pitch classes.[7] The third method (found in four or more parts) uses the final plus its upper *and* lower fifth, resulting in three different pitch classes.[8]

---

[5]Refer to Palestrina's Hymn: *Castae parentis*, page 146.

[6]During the Renaissance, pitch class B was increasingly used as a dominant in the Phrygian mode for purposes of imitation. However, the original dominant (pitch class C) continued to be used for cadential purposes.

[7]See Palestrina's Missa: *Ad fugam, Benedictus*, page 174, and Magnificat II toni: *Sicut erat*, page 144.

[8]See Palestrina's Motet: *Surrexit pastor bonus*, page 132, where Subject I is answered at the lower fifth and Subject II (based on the inversion of Subject I) is answered at the upper fifth. Also refer to the opening measures of Motet: *Anima mea turbata est*, page 139.

3.5 OTHER DISSONANCES

Black-Note Dissonances
Quarter and eighth notes in three parts are treated the same as in two parts, although perfect fourths and tritones between the upper parts may virtually be considered consonant and need no special consideration. As a general rule, moving dissonances against a stationary part must remain consonant with each other. In addition to the examples of note-against-note dissonance (i. e., the appoggiatura) illustrated in Example 2.24 on page 36, the following combined dissonances may, on occasion, be found. The illustrations shown in Example 3.19, drawn from the music of Palestrina, are by no means common. Notice that each voice, individually, is treated correctly in reference to a suitable stationary voice.

EXAMPLE 3.19 UNUSUAL DISSONANCES BETWEEN MOVING VOICES

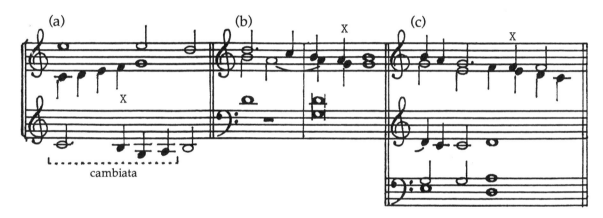

cambiata

Comments on Example 3.19:

(a) A note-against-note dissonance here combines a cambiata with an unaccented quarter-note passing tone.

(b) A ⌊9 – 8⌋ suspension resolved with an anticipation is combined here with a lower auxiliary resulting in parallel seconds and a note-against-note dissonance.

(c) An unaccented quarter-note passing tone is combined with an anticipation, producing a note-against-note dissonant combination on the resolution of a ⌊4 – 3⌋ suspension and resulting in parallel seconds.

The Consonant Fourth
Occasionally, the perfect fourth was used in the preparation of a ⌊4 – 3⌋ suspension.[9] Since suspensions are normally prepared

---

[9]See Palestrina's Missa: *Pater noster, Benedictus*, measures 9–10, page 100.

with a consonance, the appendage "consonant" is affixed to the fourth to denote this special situation. Historically, the consonant/dissonant treatment of the harmonic perfect fourth has been one of ambivalence; this practice serves as a reminder of that fact.

When used in the preparation of a ⌞4 – 3⌟ suspension, the consonant fourth (C4), moving against a bass note that is usually the value of a breve, must satisfy all of the following:

1. It must be approached by step from above or below to create a C4⁶ combination.

2. It must be held over to become the suspended fourth when a fifth above the bass is added to the suspension.

3. It must be resolved in the normal manner.

EXAMPLE 3.20   THE CONSONANT FOURTH IN THE ⌞4 – 3⌟ SUSPENSION

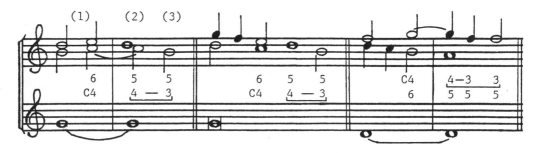

The Six-Five Chord

The ⁶₅ combination was given special treatment because of the dissonant interval of a second (or seventh) that occurs between the upper voices. This upper-voice dissonance was treated like a ⌞2 – 3⌟ (or ⌞7 – 6⌟) suspension which, on resolution, requires the bottom voice to move up by step. As with all suspensions, the ⁶₅ must occur on beats 1 or 3 and must be prepared with a consonance.[10]

Although the ⁶₅ was treated in a number of different ways, the most common form requires the fifth of the ⁶₅ to be the suspended voice.[11] Use the following procedure to write a ⁶₅ chord:

1. From a consonant preparation on beats 2 or 4, suspend one of the upper voices to become a fifth above the bass on the next beat.

2. Add the fifth (below the suspended voice) and the sixth (above the bass note) on beats 1 or 3.

---

[10]See Palestrina's Missa: *O Rex gloriae,* measure 19, page 105, and Hymn: *Virgo singularis,* measure 26, page 114.

[11]See Palestrina's Missa: *Secunda, Benedictus,* measure 22, page 119, for an alternate treatment of the six-five chord.

3. While the sixth remains stationery on the beat of resolution (2 or 4), resolve the suspended fifth down by step and move the bass up by step.

EXAMPLE 3.21   **WRITING THE SIX-FIVE CHORD**

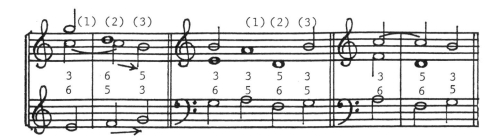

The diminished fifth becomes a prominent harmonic factor when either pitch class E or F is used as the suspended fifth. When F is used, a $\frac{6}{TT}$ combination results on the suspension beat (Example 3.22(a)). If pitch class E is suspended, a B diminished chord results on the beat of resolution (illustration (b) of Example 3.21).

This illustration presents a stylistic anomaly in that the tritone dissonance on beat two, which must be treated as a half-note passing tone because of its dissonance status, must also serve as a resolution to the $\frac{6}{5}$ chord on beat one.[12] Although it is by no means clear in this case, it is reasonable to assume that the tritone would have received a B♭ correction during performance in order to provide the expected consonant resolution to the $\frac{6}{5}$ chord. However, since beat two is not treated as a half-note passing tone in illustration (c) there is no question that a B♭ correction is needed, as shown in illustration (d).

EXAMPLE 3.22   **THE TRITONE IN THE $\frac{6}{5}$ CHORD**

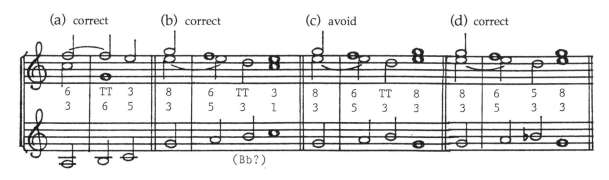

---

[12]See Palestrina's Magnificat IV toni: *Fecit potentiam*, measure 34, page 112, and Motet: *Anima mea turbata est*, measures 24–25, pages 140–141.

Although the $^6_5$ chord was not used alone in conclusive cadences, it was occasionally combined with a consonant fourth to serve as a preparation for both cadential and noncadential ⌊4 − 3⌋ suspensions.[13] To write this combination, follow the established procedure for writing a $^6_5$ chord, but on the resolution beat keep the bass stationary. A fourth results on beat 2 or 4, which serves as the preparation for the ⌊4 − 3⌋ suspension. Be sure that the C4 preparation is a *perfect* fourth.

EXAMPLE 3.23   **(a) THE $^6_5$ AS AN ADJUNCT TO A ⌊4 − 3⌋ SUSPENSION**

(b) THE $^6_5$ AS AN ADJUNCT TO A ⌊4 − 3⌋ CONCLUSIVE CADENCE

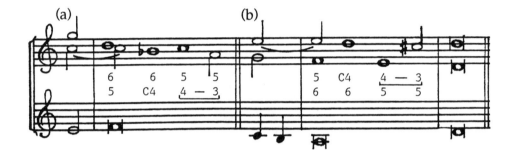

---

[13]See Palestrina's Missa: *Secunda, Benedictus*, measure 16, page 119, and Lamentation: *Feria VI, Lectio III, Vetustam fecit*, measures 101–102, page 166.

4 Counterpoint in Four and Five Parts

4.1 WRITING MULTIPLE-VOICED WORKS

All the stylistic principles and contrapuntal devices covered in three-part writing apply equally to multiple-voice composition. Problems of voice leading, obviously, become more complex and require special attention. In addition to careful and thoughtful analysis, reducing multiple-voice scores to two or three staves for purposes of study can be helpful.

Texture   Although rests in three-part works are used primarily for cadential punctuation and textual clarification, they also are used to reduce the number of parts to create textural contrast and subtle changes in tone color. These periodic reductions serve the same functions in multiple-voice works as well. In addition, fluctuations in the number of parts also helps to create textural contrast with homophonic sections where full scoring is normally preferred.

The charts in Example 4.1 illustrate the extent to which rests (shown as clear boxes) can be used to vary the texture in multiple-voiced works. Illustration (a) shows a fluctuation in the number of voices from four to two and three parts.[1] Similar fluctuations

---

[1]Refer to Palestrina's Motet: *Exaudi Domine*, measures 5–35, pages 124–126.

can be seen in illustration (b), where a five-voiced texture is periodically reduced to three and four parts.[2] The regularity with which rests occur in this movement is due to its canonic structure. However, the treatment of the text in regard to the use of rests should be carefully studied.

EXAMPLE 4.1   THE USE OF RESTS IN MULTIPLE-VOICED TEXTURES

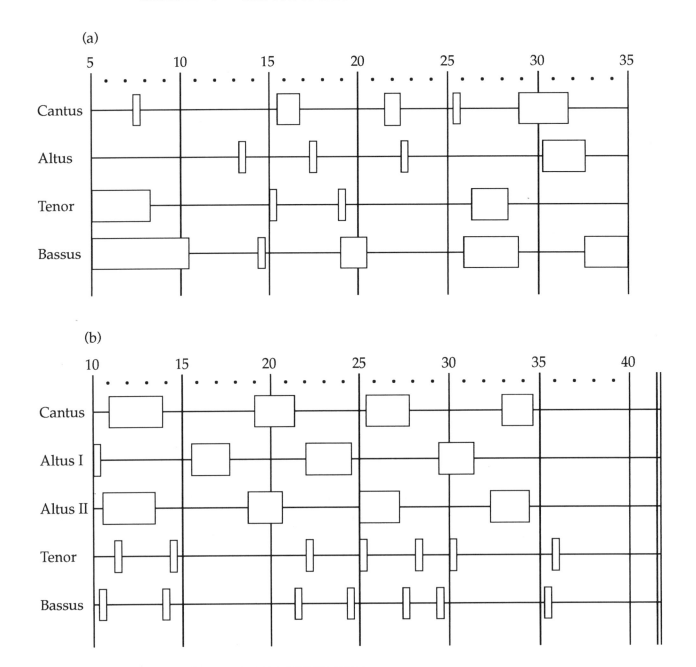

_____

[2]See Palestrina's Missa: *Ad fugam, Agnus Dei II*, measures 10–40, pages 176–179.

Familiar Style   Familiar style, found in both triple and $\frac{4}{2}$ meter, was used in short, contrasting sections as well as in whole movements. Chords related by one common tone (fifth related) occur about twice as frequently in this style as do chords related by two common tones or chords with no tones in common.

The use of *musica ficta* in familiar style may be expanded to include changes in chord quality, but avoid superimposing tonal over modal functions with these changes. B♭ may be used to alter chords when forming part of the A–B♭–A melodic sequence (in chord progressions such as d–B♭–a and F–g–d) and C♯, F♯, and G♯ may be used to create "dominant" effects (such as D–G, D–C, or A–D–G), providing these alterations are used with discretion.

4.2 SUSPENSIONS AND CADENCES

Suspensions   While bass-note doublings should be given preference in upper-voice suspensions, any chord member other than the suspension voice may be doubled. In five or more parts, bass doublings in the ⌊9 – 8⌋ suspension (Example 4.2(g)) tend to be less frequent than with other types of upper-voice suspensions.

EXAMPLE 4.2   Doublings in common suspensions

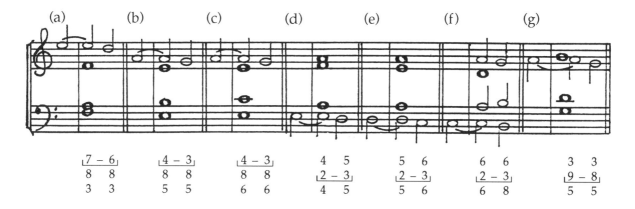

Suspensions that include complete seventh chords are illustrated in Example 4.3. Notice in illustration (c) of Example 4.3 that the added voice in the $\frac{6}{5}$ chord causes no change in its usual treatment.

EXAMPLE 4.3   SUSPENSIONS THAT INCLUDE COMPLETE SEVENTH CHORDS

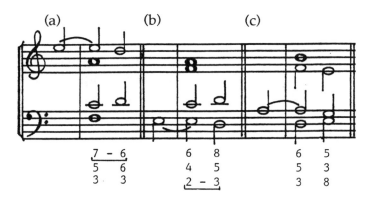

Conclusive Cadences

The two most frequently used conclusive cadences in multiple-voiced works were the ⌊4 – 3⌋ and plagal cadences. Although the ⌊7 – 6⌋ conclusive cadence may occasionally be found, especially in works in the Phrygian mode, the ⌊2 – 3⌋ conclusive cadence was seldom used for this purpose.

EXAMPLE 4.4   THE ⌊4 – 3⌋ CONCLUSIVE CADENCE IN FOUR VOICES

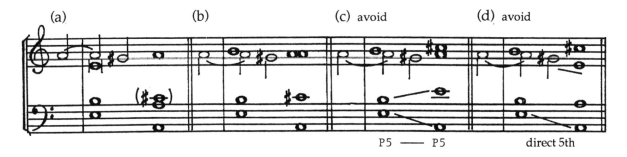

EXAMPLE 4.5   THE PLAGAL CADENCE IN FOUR VOICES

EXAMPLE 4.6   **(a) AND (b) THE ⌊4 – 3⌋ CONCLUSIVE CADENCE IN FIVE VOICES**
(c) – (e) THE PLAGAL CADENCE IN FIVE VOICES

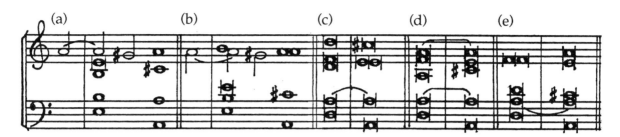

Make note of the doublings and voice leading in the Phrygian cadence in illustrations (b) and (c) of Example 4.7. In contrast to other ⌊7 – 6⌋ conclusive cadences, it is important *not* to double the bass in the Phrygian cadence.

EXAMPLE 4.7   **(a) AND (b) THE ⌊7 – 6⌋ CONCLUSIVE CADENCE IN FOUR VOICES**
(c) AND (d) THE ⌊7 – 6⌋ CONCLUSIVE CADENCE IN FIVE VOICES

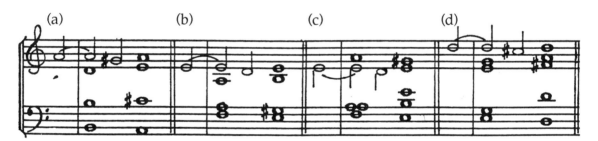

In addition to the conclusive cadences discussed in the preceding examples, the following cadential extensions (Examples 4.8 and 4.9) are frequently found. The final or dominant is used as a pedal in these cadential extensions and, although no particular preference is evident in common-tone progressions, the penultimate and final chords are always related by one common tone resulting in a "V–I" or "IV–I" cadence. In cadences of an authentic type, the fifth of the final chord is tied; in the plagal cadence, it is the final that is tied throughout. All illustrations are from Palestrina's works.

EXAMPLE 4.8   (a) AUTHENTIC CADENCE IN FOUR VOICES
(b) PLAGAL CADENCE IN FOUR VOICES

(a)

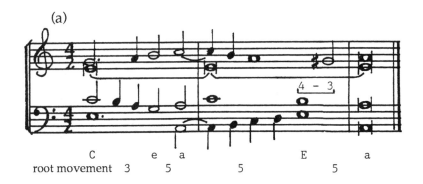

```
                C      e    a            E        a
root movement   3      5         5       5
```

(b)

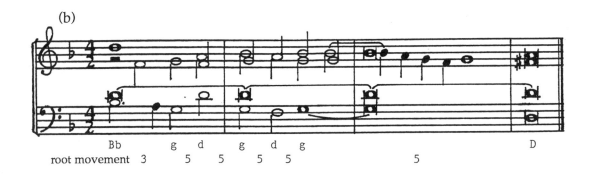

```
                Bb     g    d    g    d    g                D
root movement   3      5    5    5    5              5
```

EXAMPLE 4.9   (a) AUTHENTIC CADENCE IN FIVE VOICES
(b) PLAGAL CADENCE IN FIVE VOICES

(a)

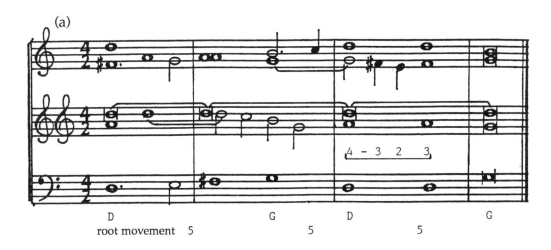

```
                D                 G    D              G
root movement   5                 5             5
```

(b)

root movement

4.3 TRIPLE METER

Triple-note groupings occur in $\frac{3}{2}$ and $\frac{3}{1}$ meter.[3] In $\frac{3}{2}$ meter, the dotted whole note receives the beat. In $\frac{3}{1}$ meter (where the breve equals three whole notes), either the whole note receives the beat ("slow meter") or the breve receives the beat ("fast meter"). Tempo actually remains relatively constant, but the speed of note values varies due to changes in their proportional value. A "slow" $\frac{3}{1}$ meter is treated as a $\frac{6}{2}$ meter (i. e., like a $\frac{4}{2}$ meter plus two additional half notes), with suspensions occurring on beats 1, 3, or 5 and half-note passing tones on beats 2, 4, or 6.

EXAMPLE 4.10   THE "SLOW" $\frac{3}{1}$ METER

---

[3]For an example of triple meter in three parts see Palestrina's Missa: *Ave Regina coelorum, Crucifixus*, measures 23–34, page 122; in four parts, Missa: *Ad fugam, Hosanna*, page 172; in five parts, Offertory: *Deus enim firmavit*, measures 31–42, page 152.

The "fast" $\frac{3}{1}$ meter is characterized by the treatment of notes in diminutive values approximating one-half their usual notational value. Notice, in Example 4.11, that the half note is used as an auxiliary and an anticipation, and that quarter notes are treated as eighth notes. The hemiola effect in the first example is a common occurrence.

EXAMPLE *4.11*   THE "FAST" $\frac{3}{1}$ METER

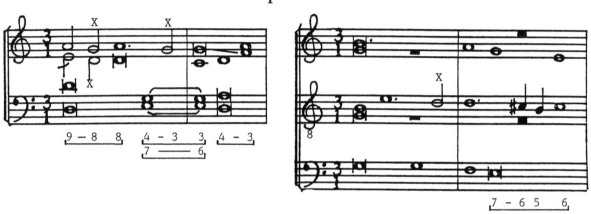

The relatively rapid white-note movement in triple meter resulted in a greater use of homorhythmic texture and in a reduction in the use of black-note dissonances. Consequently, the placement of the suspension dissonance was treated with greater flexibility. Notice in Example 4.12, which is in $\frac{3}{2}$ meter, as in Example 4.11, that there is a lack of variety in black-note activity and that suspensions occur on all beats.

EXAMPLE *4.12*   THE $\frac{3}{2}$ METER

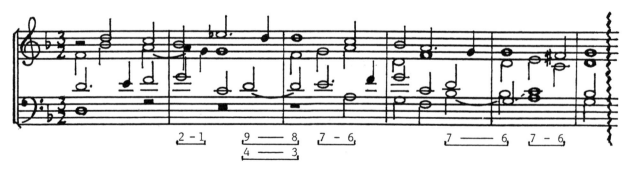

4.4 GUIDELINES

The following observations and guidelines may prove helpful when writing multiple-voiced works.

1. As a general rule, when moving parts in quarter notes are dissonant with each other, they must, individually, be treated correctly against a suitable stationary voice (refer to Example 3.17, page 59).

2. Restrictions on downward skips from off-beats and the use of upper auxiliaries may be eased somewhat. Notice, however, the motive significance of these exceptions as well as their rare occurrence.[4]

3. Overlap voices in interior cadential areas to enhance a continuous sonic flow of the texture. In this regard, complete cadential closure usually occurs only before entering sections in familiar style and/or triple meter, at the conclusion of large sections, or for specific textual reasons.

4. Because Palestrina's works are so solidly based on the technique of imitative polyphony so characteristic of most Renaissance sacred music, the frequent use of interior cadences followed by new points of imitation should be considered a stylistic norm. However, these cadences and imitative re-entries should be based on the phrase structure of the text.

5. Balance the use of previously heard motives and imitative themes with new or developed material.

6. Except at cadence points, guard against a bass part that becomes harmonically functional rather than remaining an equal melodic partner to the upper voices.

7. Do not overlook the importance of textual fluctuations, as discussed in the beginning of this chapter and as illustrated in Example 4.1, page 66.

8. In addition to the basic approach to writing used throughout the text, alternate methods that could prove helpful are illustrated in Appendix II, Worksheets 11–13.

---

[4]See Palestrina's Magnificat V toni: *Et exsultavit*, pages 130–131 and Missa: *Ad fugam, Benedictus*, pages 174–175.

APPENDIX A

Examples for Musical Analysis

Examples Grouped by Number of Voices

The author's goal in compiling this anthology was to provide a representative cross-section of Palestrina's ecclesiastical compositions for study and analysis. For easy reference, the selected pieces are grouped below according to the number of voices used in each example. Additionally, the pieces within each group are arranged according to the increasing complexity of the writing, based on the variety and scope of dissonance, rhythmic complexity, and treatment of contrapuntal devices found in each work. Exceptions (such as the six-five chord and consonant fourth found in the concluding measures of *Vetustam fecit*) will occasionally be encountered but, generally, the organizational format should prove to be very useful. The sylistic consistency of the two-part works by Lassus precluded the need for a similar arrangement of those pieces.

Two-Part Works by Lassus (from *Cantiones darum vocum*)

Three-Part Works by Palestrina

Four-Part Works by Palestrina

Five-Part Works by Palestrina

Multiple-Movement Works by Palestrina

Works By Lassus
(from *Cantiones darum vocum*)

Beatus vir

Lassus

Oculus non vidit

Lassus

Justus cor suum tradet

Lassus

Ex spectatio justorum

Lassus

Justi tulerunt

Lassus

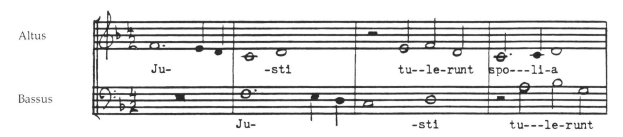

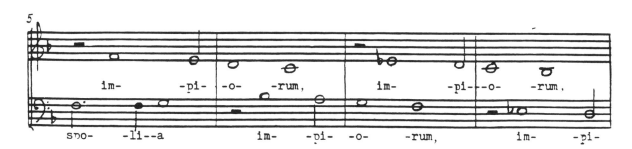

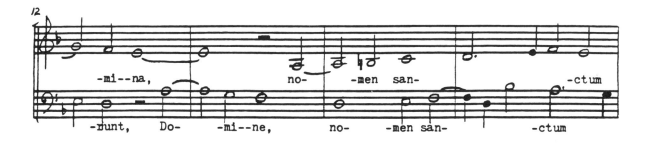

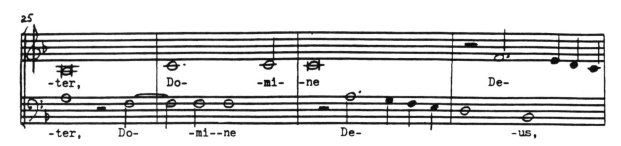

Sancti mei

Lassus

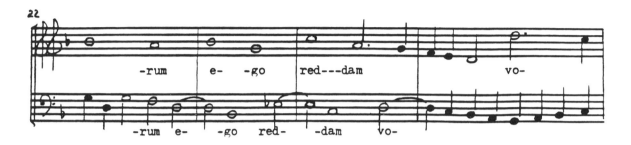

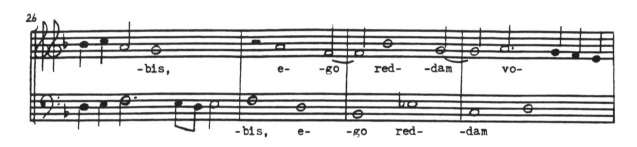

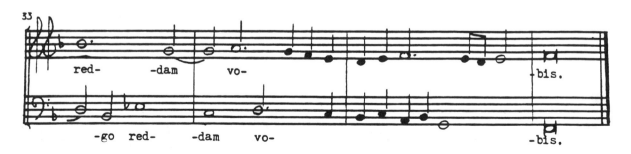

Serve bone

Lassus

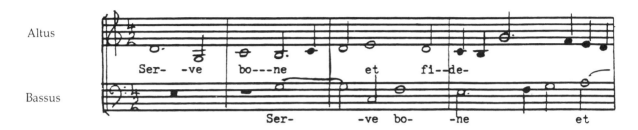

18

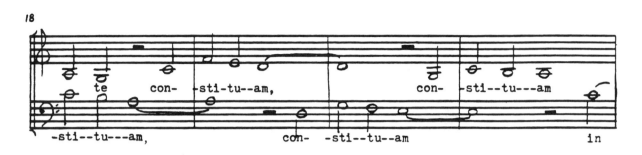

22

26

30

33

WORKS BY PALESTRINA

Lamentation: *Feria VI in parasceve*
Lectio II, Filii Sion

Palestrina

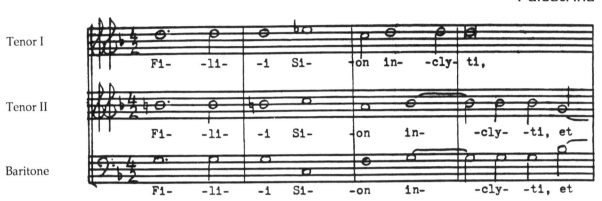

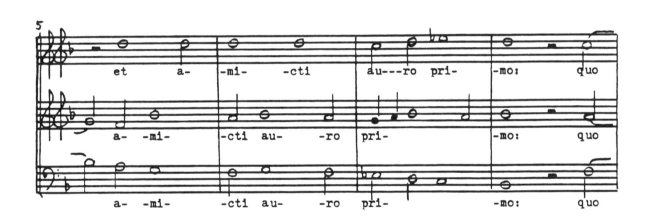

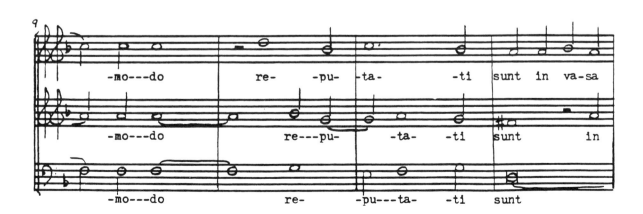

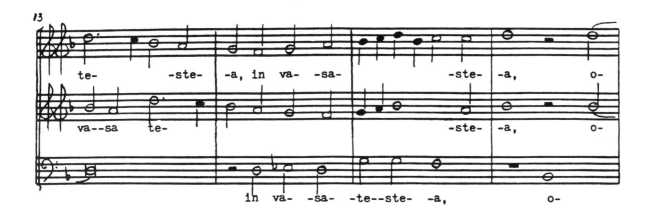

Missa: *Tertia, Jesu nostra redemptio*
Benedictus

Palestrina

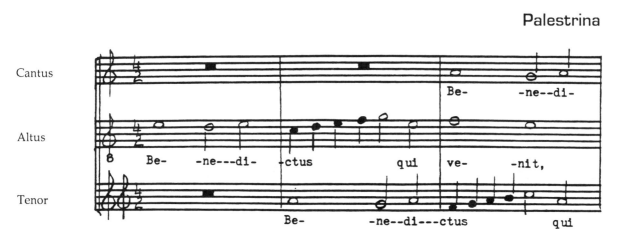

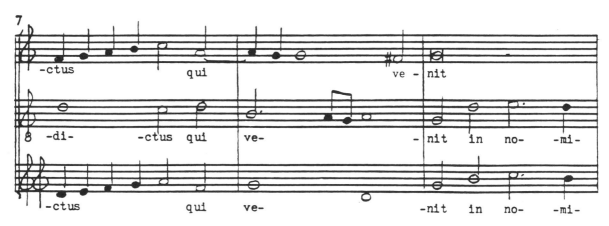

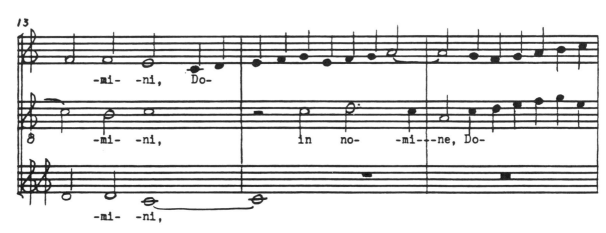

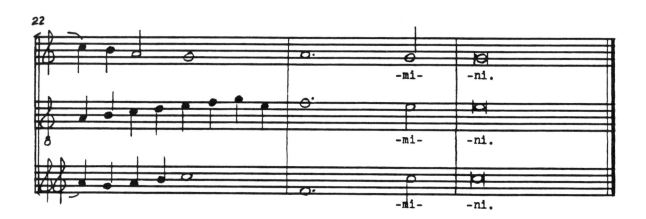

Missa: *Veni sponsa Christi*
Pleni sunt coeli[1]

Palestrina

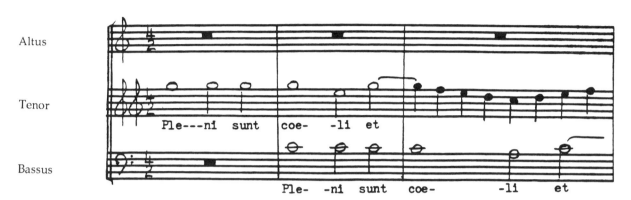

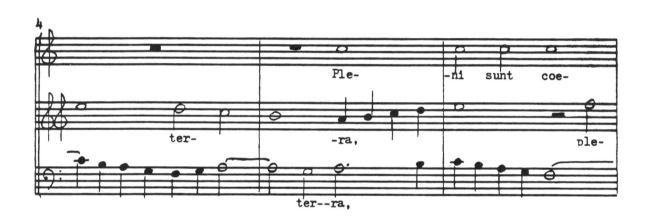

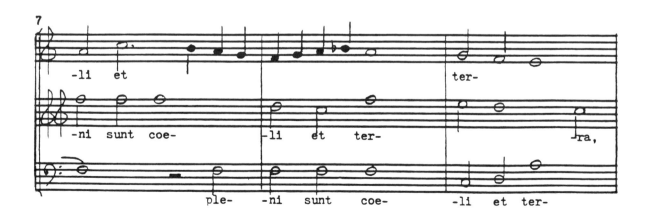

---

[1]*Pleni sunt coeli* is a subsection of the Sanctus movement.

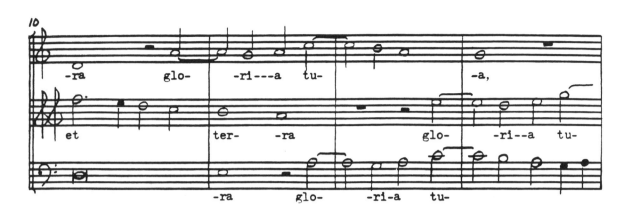

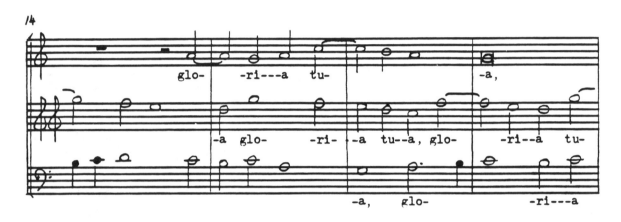

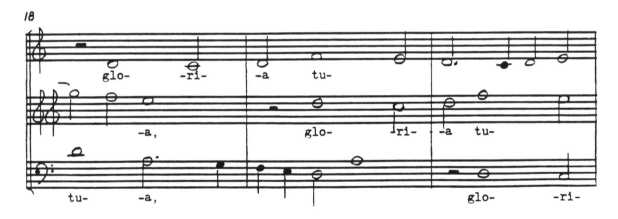

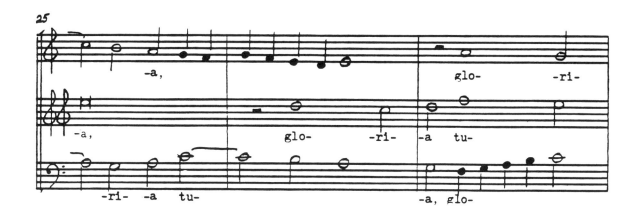

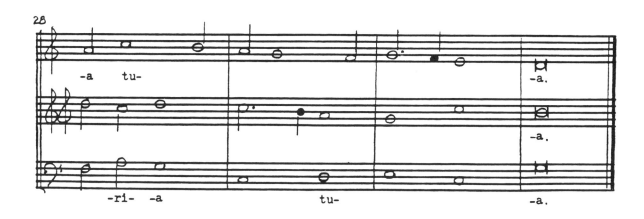

Missa: *Pater noster*
Benedictus

Palestrina

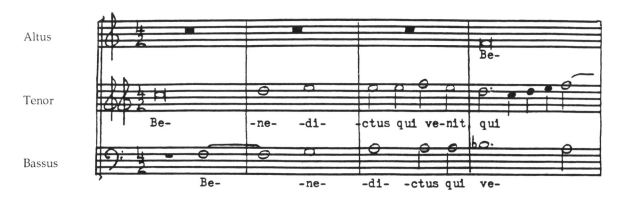

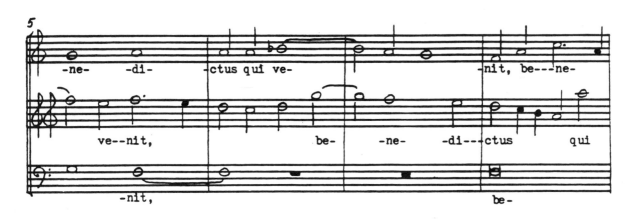

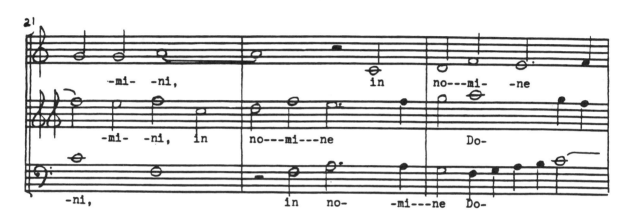

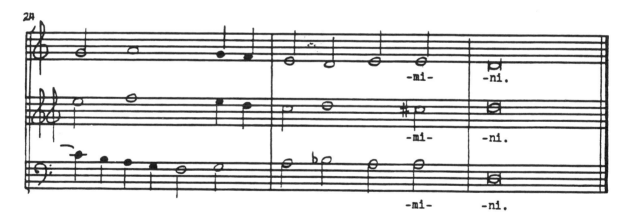

Missa: *Quarta (L'Homme armé)*
Benedictus

Palestrina

Cantus

Altus

Tenor

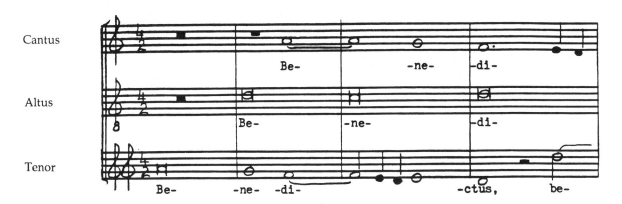

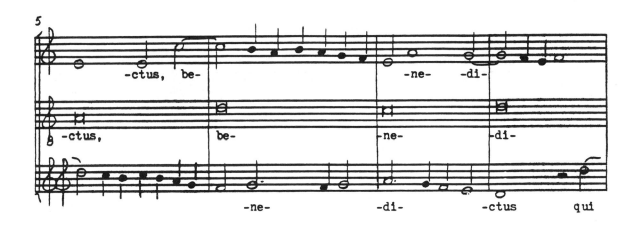

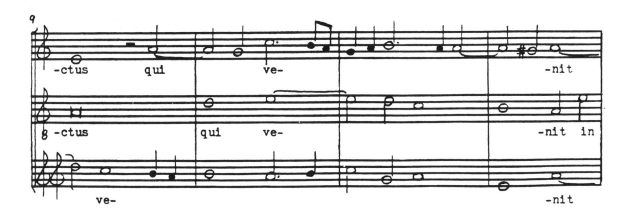

Missa: *O Rex gloriae*
Benedictus

Palestrina

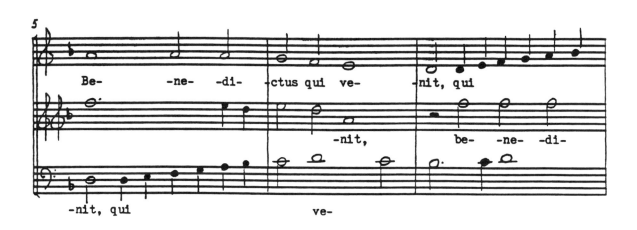

---

[2]Resolutio: identifies the voice in which the imitation will occur.

[3]Canon: identifies the voice to be imitated: the leader in the canon.

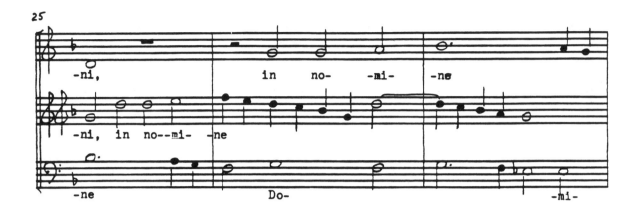

Missa: *Ave Maria*
Pleni sunt coeli

Palestrina

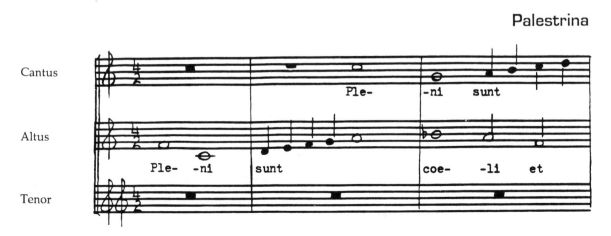

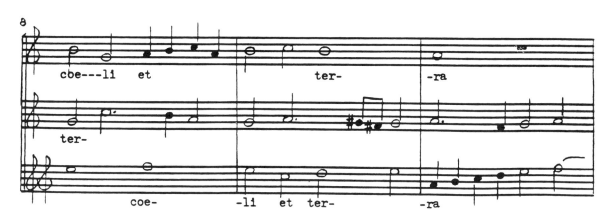

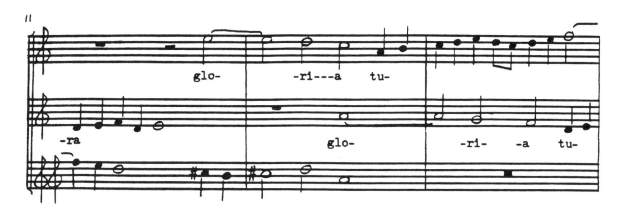

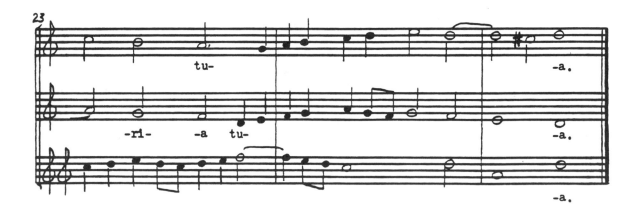

Magnificat IV toni
Fecit potentiam

Palestrina

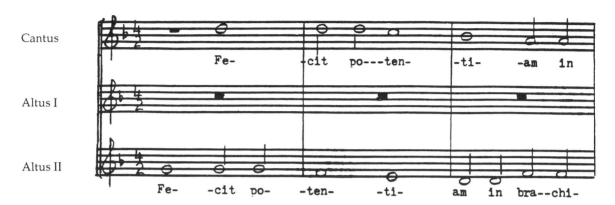

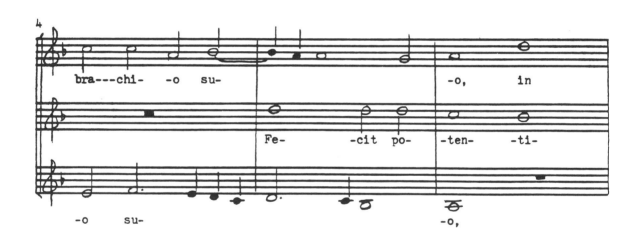

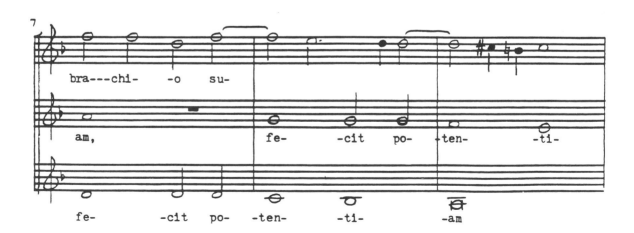

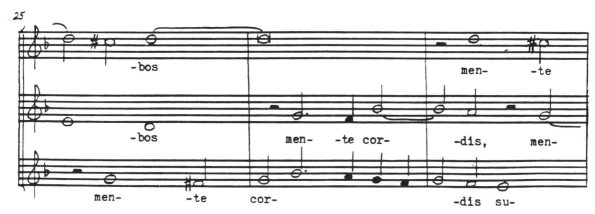

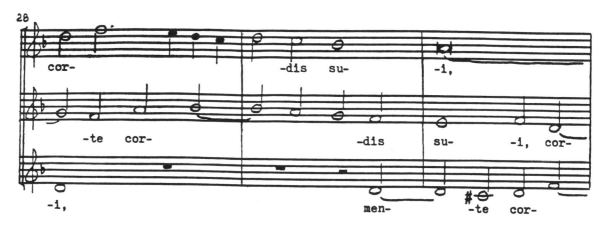

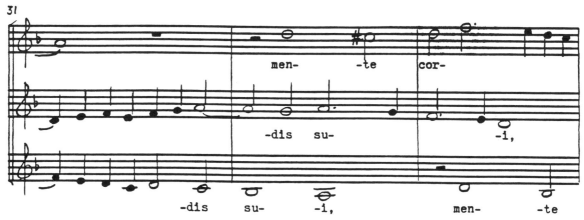

Hymn: *Virgo singularis*

Palestrina

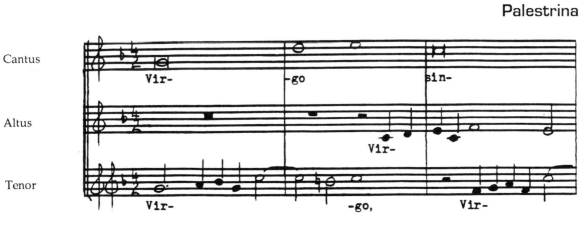

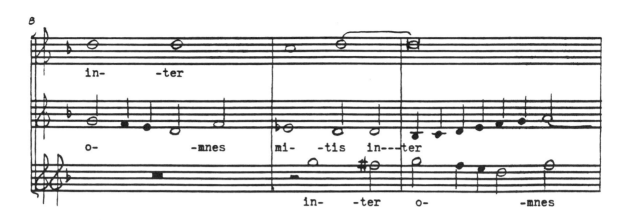

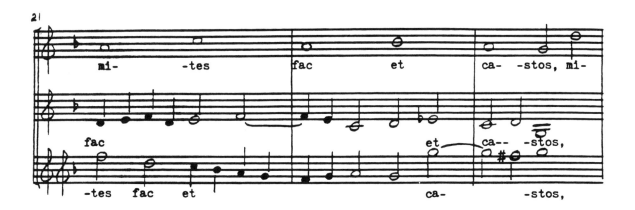

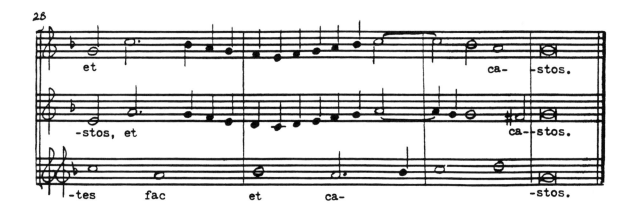

Hymn: *Lavacra puri*

Palestrina

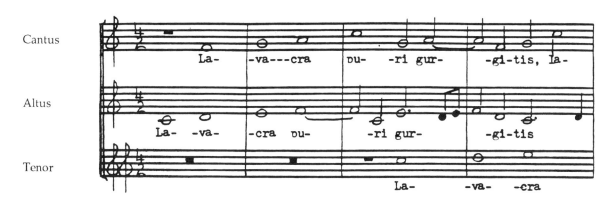

Missa: *Secunda*
Benedictus

Palestrina

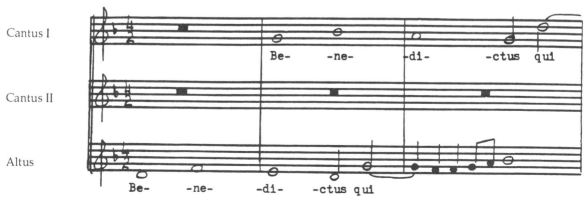

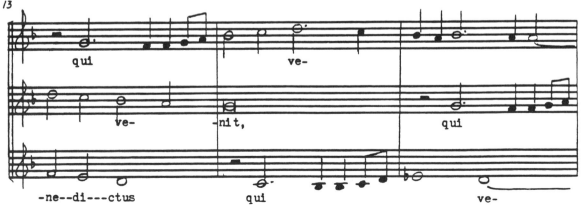

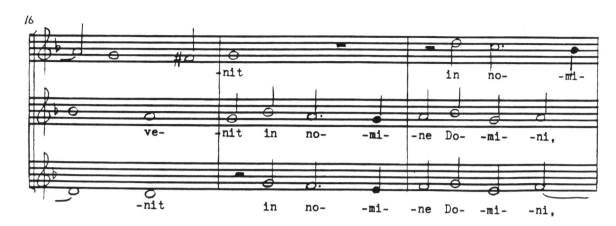

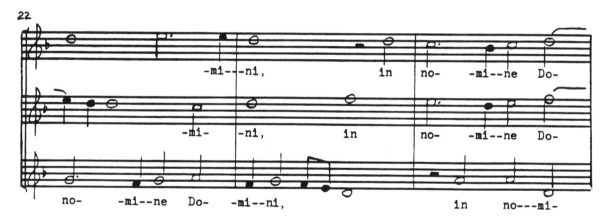

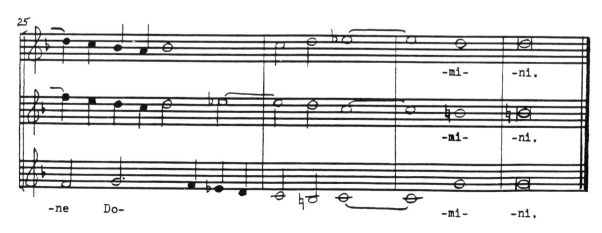

Missa: *Ave Regina coelorum*
Crucifixus[4]

Palestrina

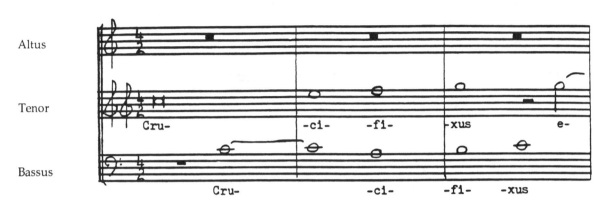

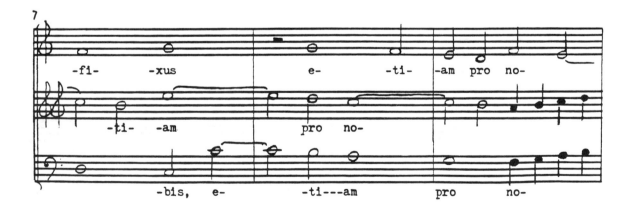

---

[4]*Crucifixus* is a subsection of the Credo movement.

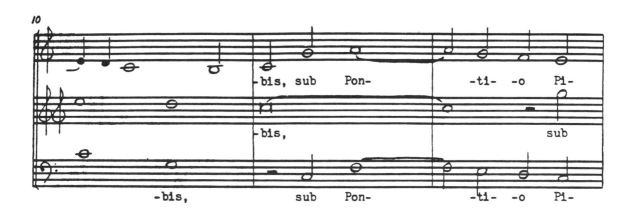

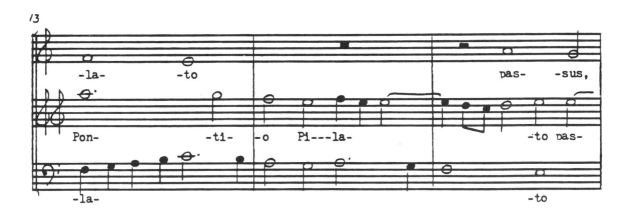

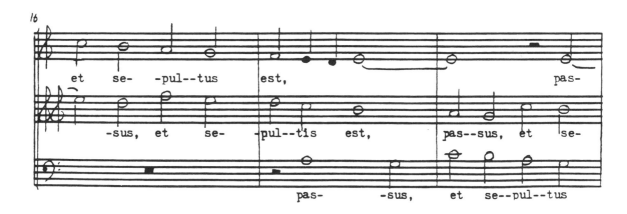

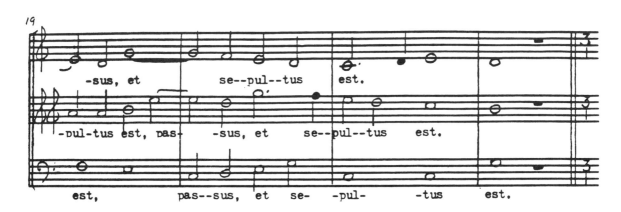

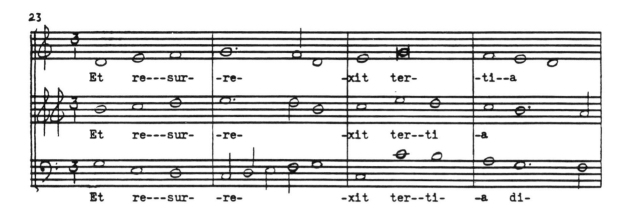

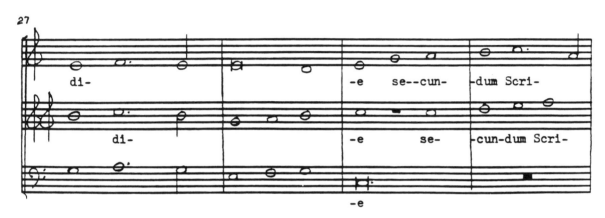

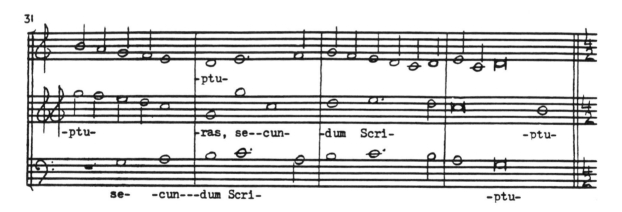

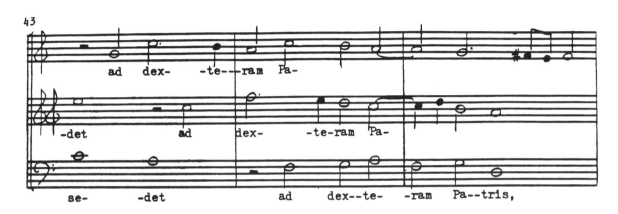

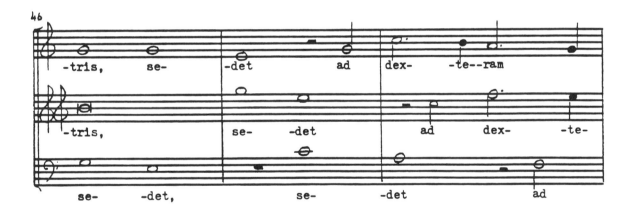

Motet: *Exaudi Domine*

Palestrina

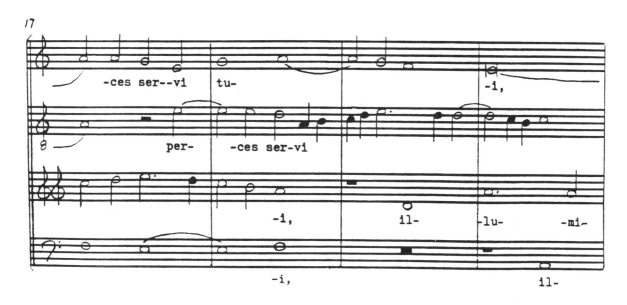

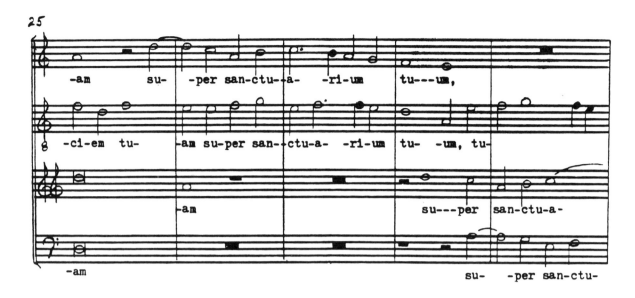

53

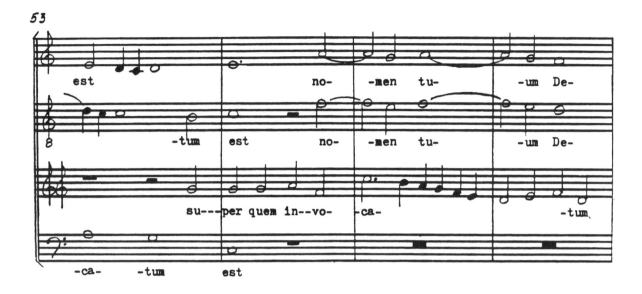

57

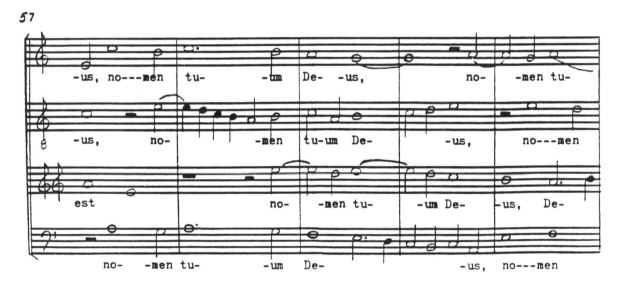

62

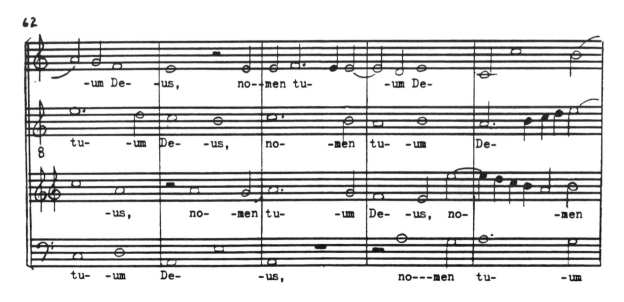

67

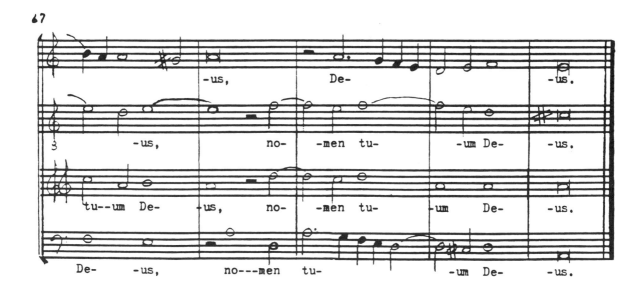

Magnificat V toni
Et exsultavit

Palestrina

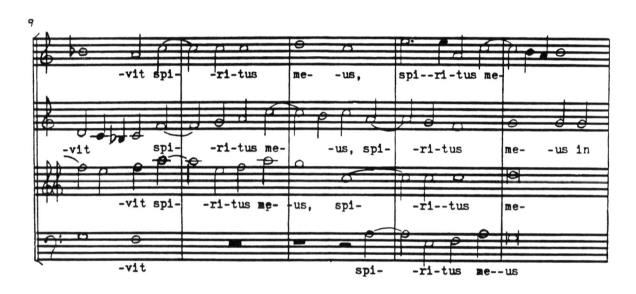

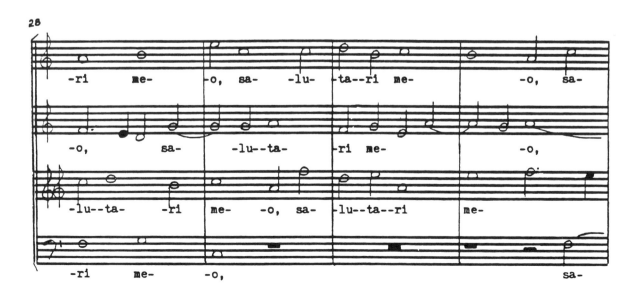

32.

Motet: *Surrexit pastor bonus*

Palestrina

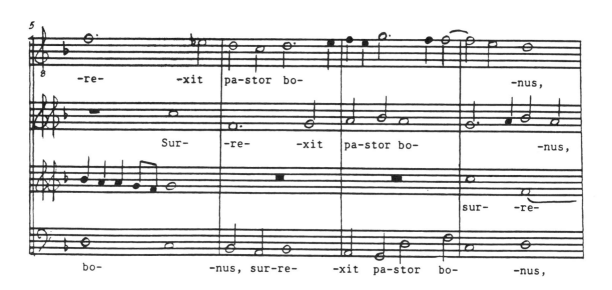

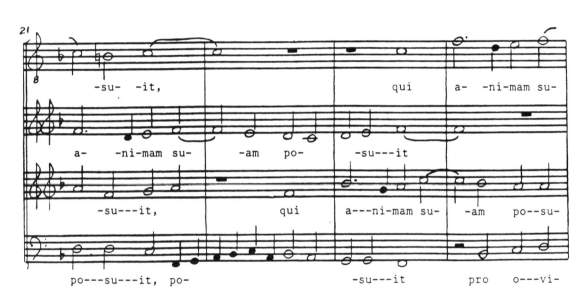

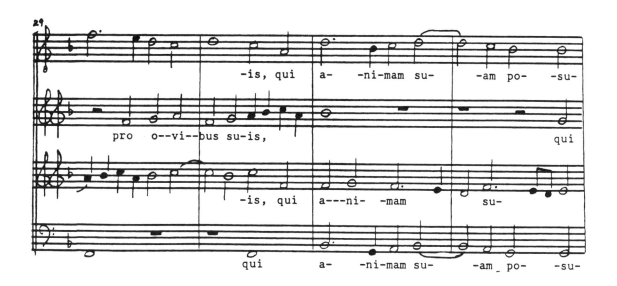

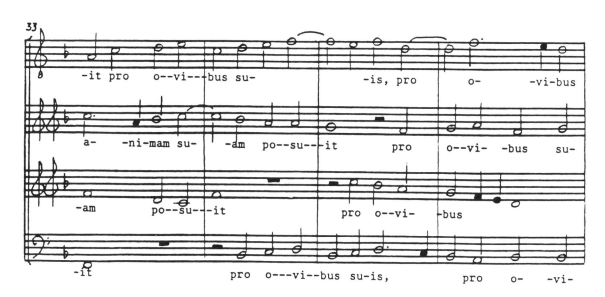

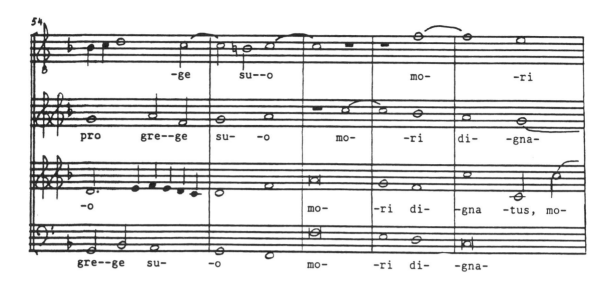

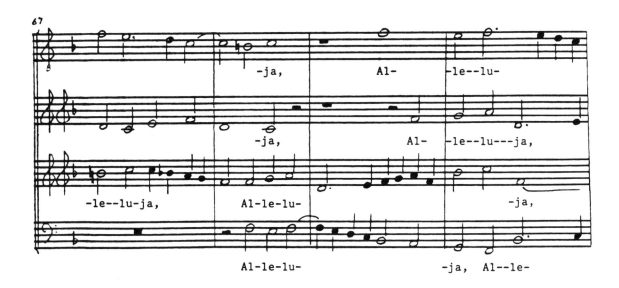

Motet: *Anima mea turbata est*

Palestrina

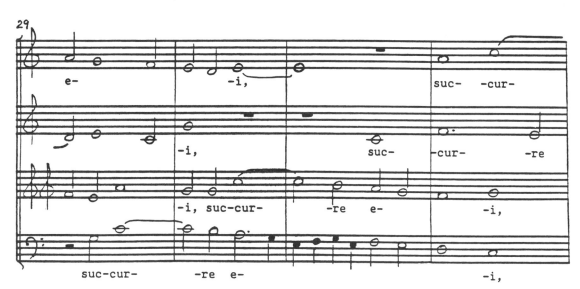

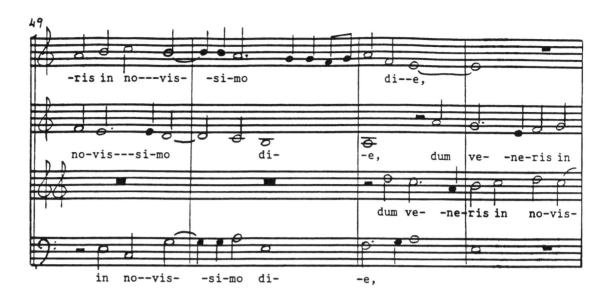

Magnificat II toni
Sicut erat

Palestrina

Hymn: *Castae parentis*

Palestrina

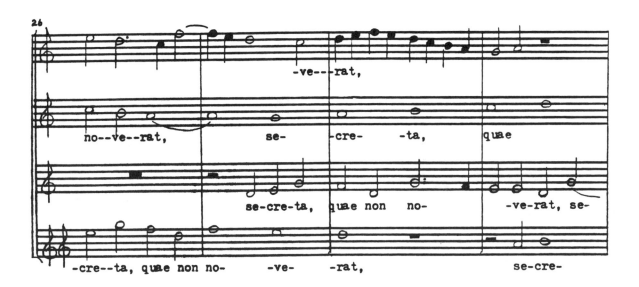

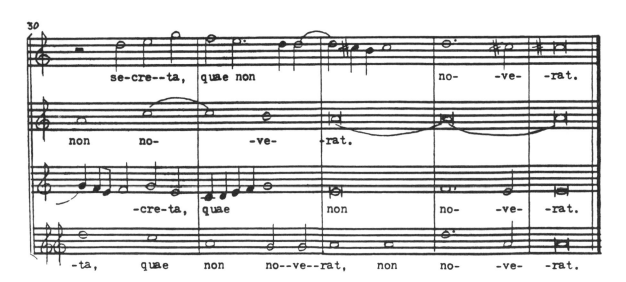

Offertory
Deus enim firmavit

Palestrina

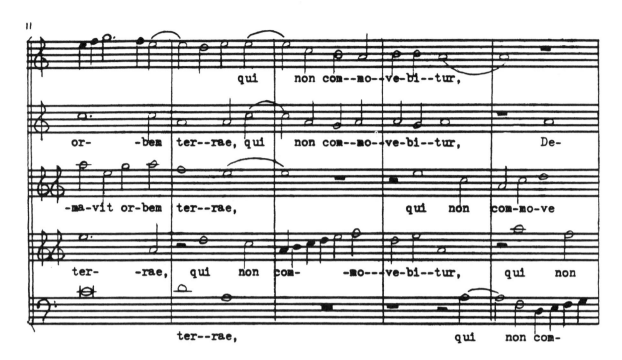

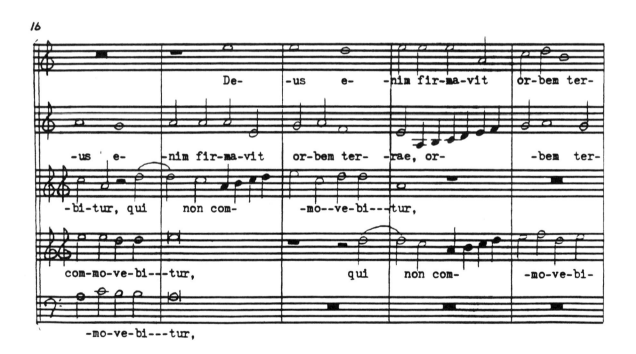

31

37

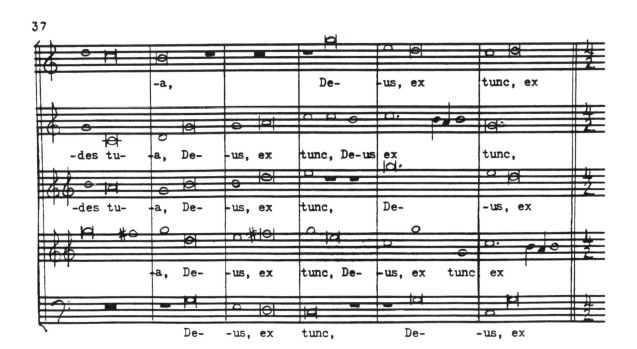

53

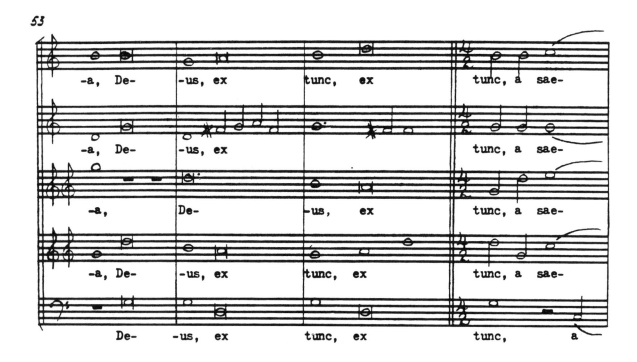

57

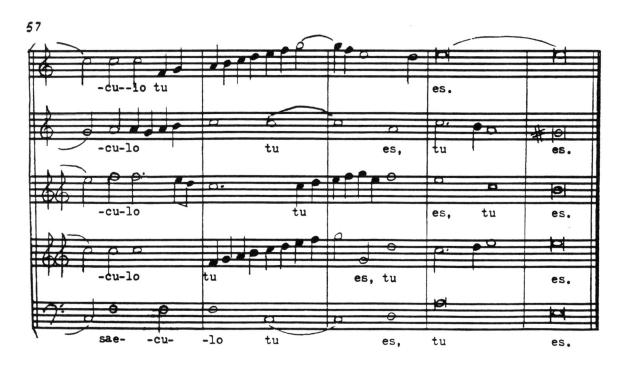

Missa: *L'Homme armé*
Kyrie (excerpt)

Palestrina

---

[5]The L'Homme armé theme occurs in its original triple meter in Tenor I, creating a two-against-three cross rhythm with the other parts. The whole note receives a triple subdivision $\left(\mathbf{o} = \text{♩♩♩}\right)$ in Tenor I, and a duple subdivision $\left(\mathbf{o} = \text{♩♩}\right)$ in the remaining parts.

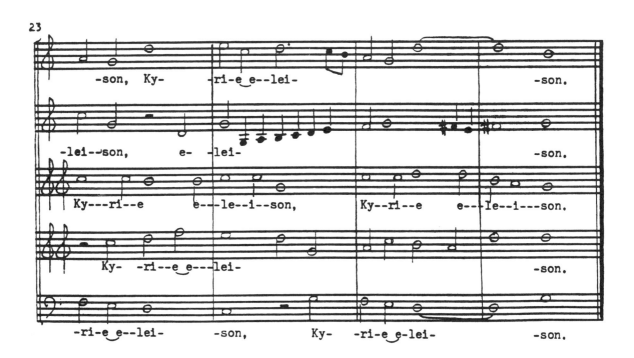

Lamentation: *Feria VI in parasceve*
Lectio III
Aleph, Ego vir, Aleph

Palestrina

Altus I

Altus II

Tenor I

Tenor II

Bassus

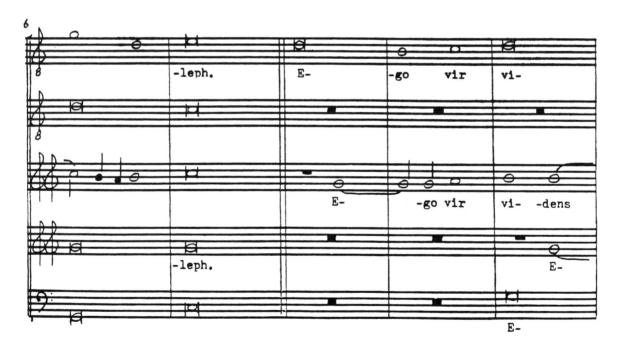

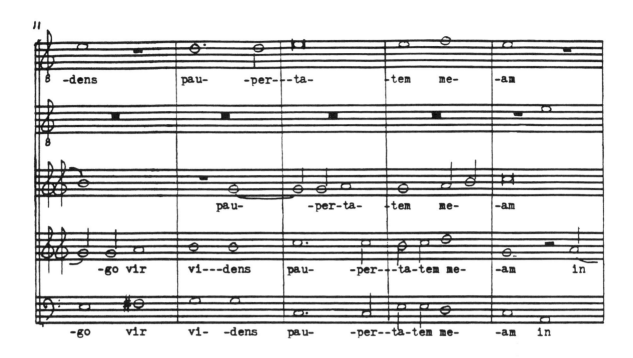

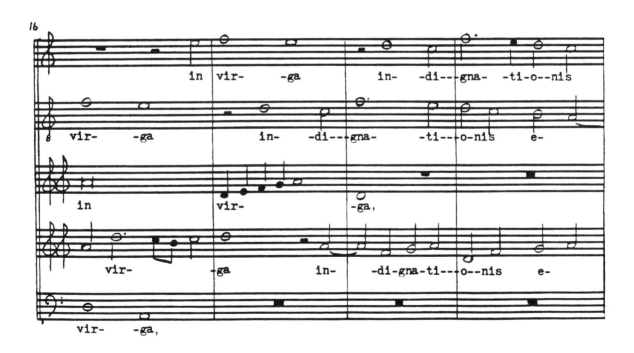

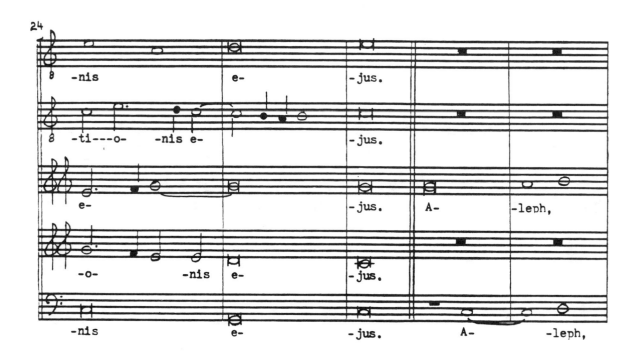

Me minavit

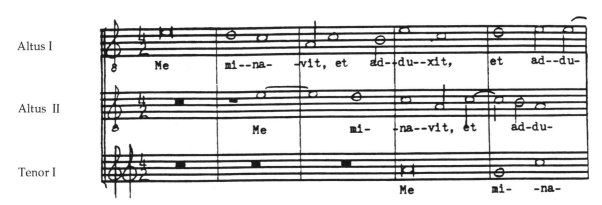

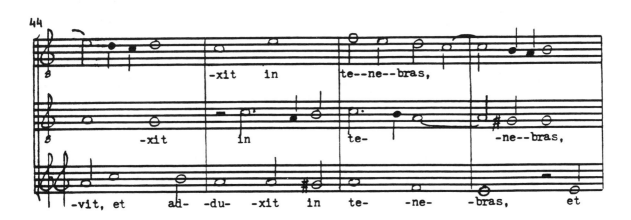

Aleph

Tantum in me vertit

Beth

Vetustam fecit

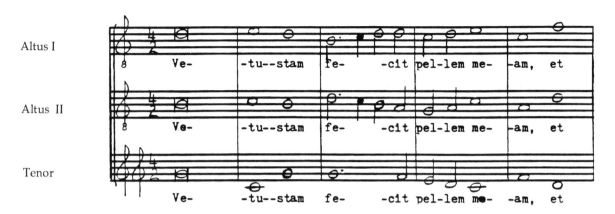

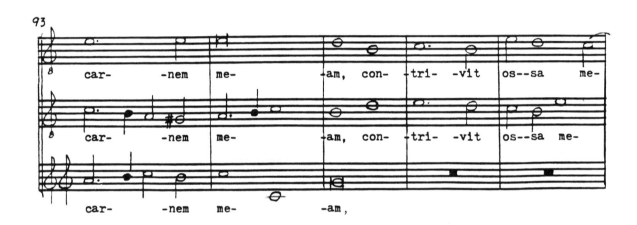

Jerusalem

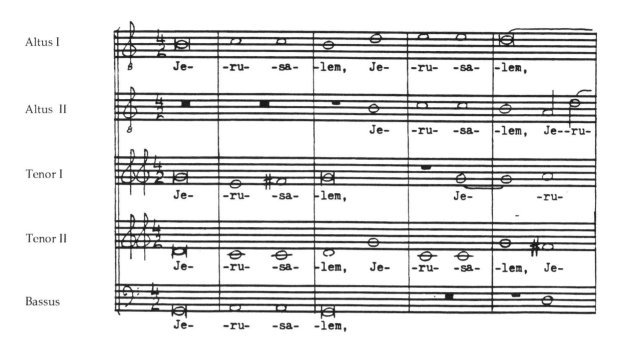

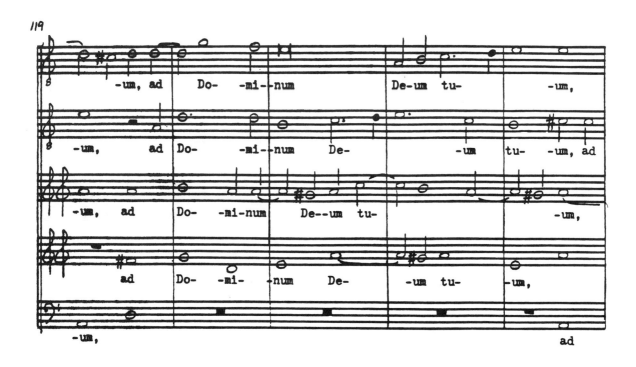

124

ad Do--mi- -num De- -um tu- -um.

Do- -mi- -num De- -um tu- -um.

ad Do-mi--num De--um tu- -um.

ad Do- -mi-num De- -um tu- -um.

Do- -mi- -num De- -um tu- -um.

Missa: *Ad fugam*
Kyrie

Palestrina

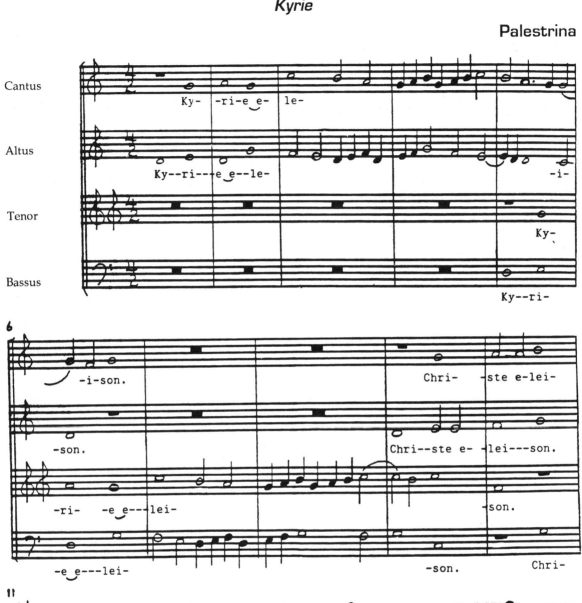

Sanctus

9

13

Hosanna

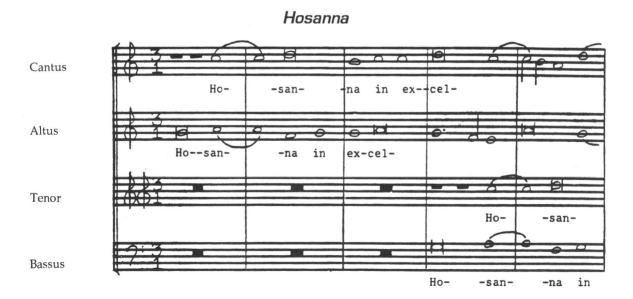

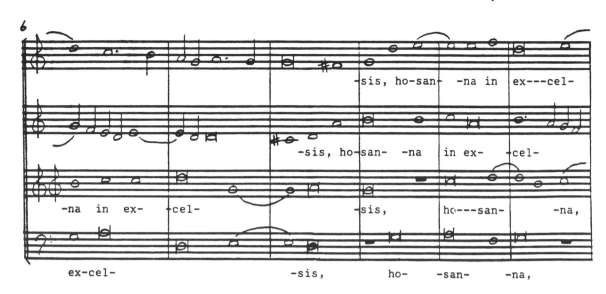

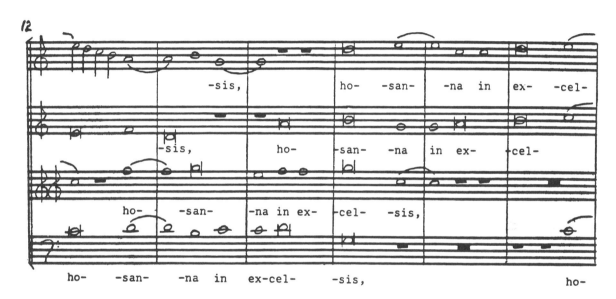

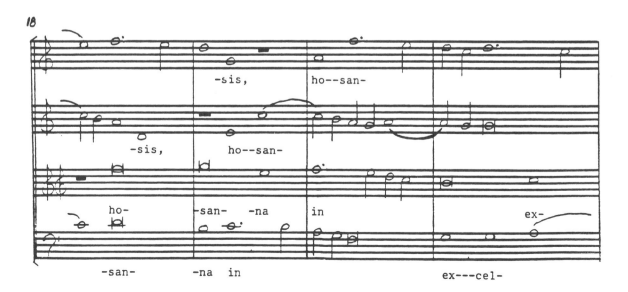

22

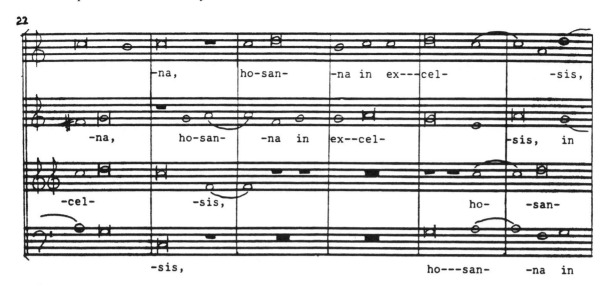

23

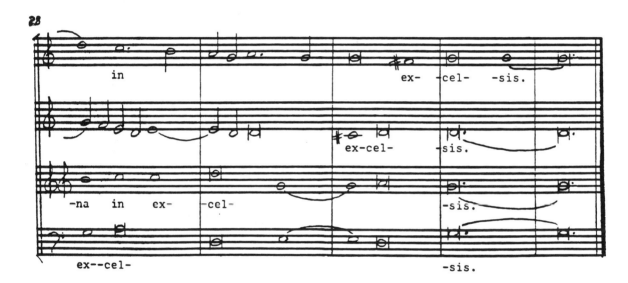

Benedictus

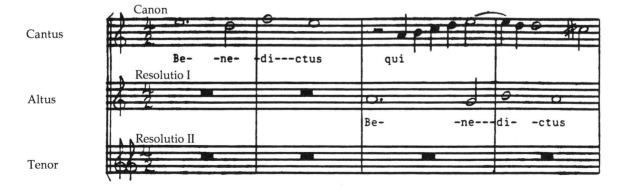

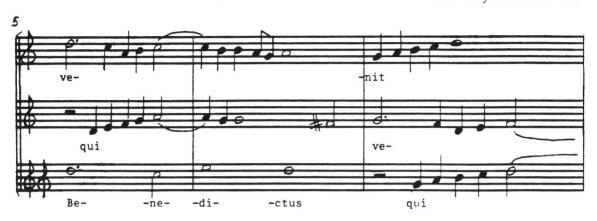
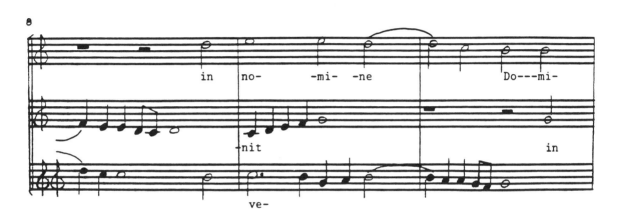
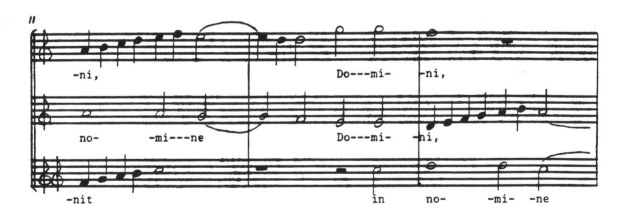

Agnus Dei II

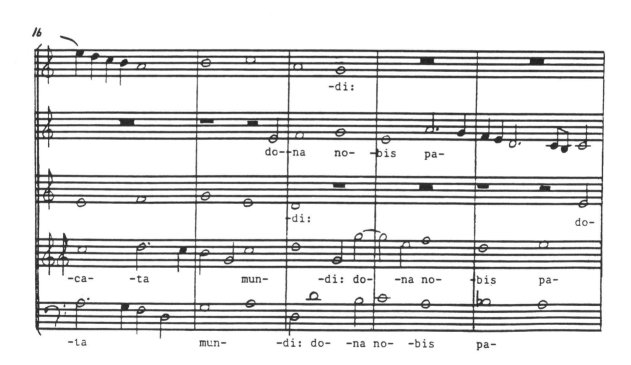

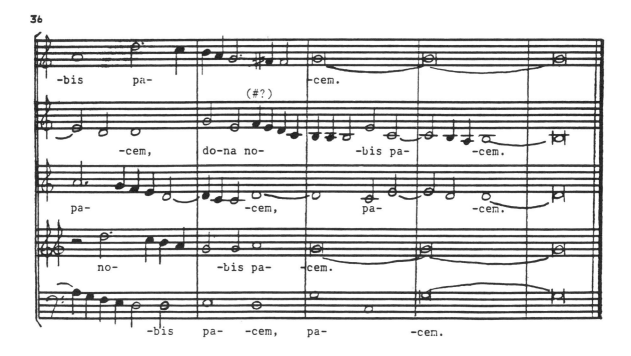

Litaniae Liber Secundus, *Prima pars* (condensed)
Kyrie eleison

Palestrina

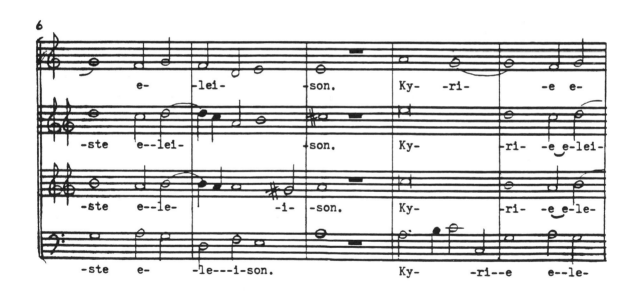

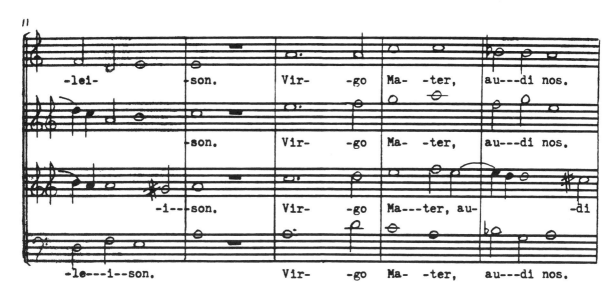

26

30

34

152

-na Sanc-cto-rum o---mni--um, o---ra pro no- -bis.

-na Sanc-cto-rum o- -mni-um, o--ra pro no- -bis.

-na San-cto--rum o- -mni--um, o--ra pro no---bis.

-na San----cto-rum o--mni- -um, o- -ra pro no- -bis.

Ave Maria

Altus

Tenor I

A- -ve Ma- -ri- -a, a-

Tenor II

A---ve Ma- -ri- -a, a-

Bassus

A- -ve

5

A- -ve Ma- -ri- -a,

-ve Ma- -ri-

-ve Ma- -ri-

Ma- -ri- -a, a- -ve Ma- -ri-

60

APPENDIX B

Written Exercises

Worksheet (W–1)
Melody

1. Complete the following using white-note values in appropriate stepwise movement.

2. Use each of the skipping patterns below in three short melodies. Use white-note values only, one pattern per melody.

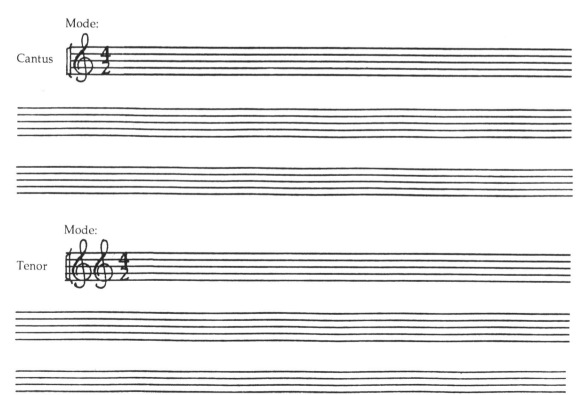

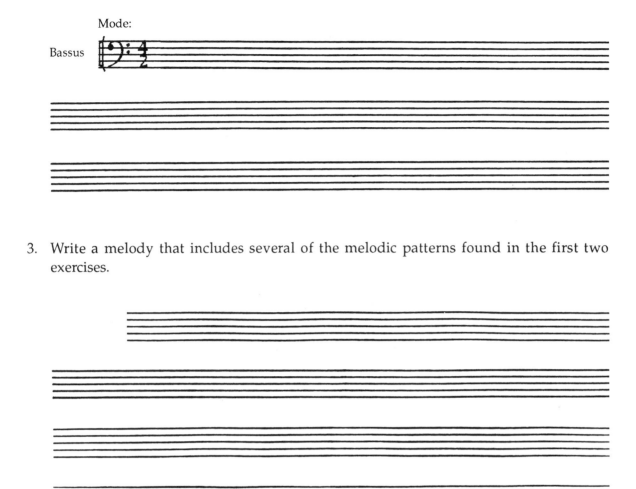

Mode:

Bassus

3. Write a melody that includes several of the melodic patterns found in the first two exercises.

4. Locate and identify at least 10 mistakes in the following melody.

Aeolian

Cantus

Worksheet (W–2)
Melody

1. Use a cambiata and at least one anticipation in a short melody.

Mode:

Altus

2. Write a short melody that includes several examples of quarter-note skips.

Mode:

Bassus

3. Write a melody that includes the following rhythmic patterns.

Mode:

Cantus

4. Write a melody that includes several of the melodic patterns discussed in Chapter 1 on pages 14–17.

5. Write a melody similar to the preceding exercise with text. Set line 4a (Sanctus, etc.) from page 21. Rests may be used to divide the melody into two or three phrases.

Worksheet (W–3)
Two-Part Counterpoint

1. Add a Cantus part in whole notes and breves using consonances only.

2. Write a Bassus part to the Tenor using consonances only. Remember, the Tenor sounds one octave lower than written.

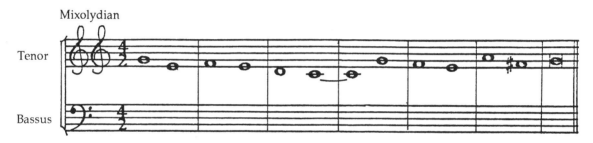

3. Locate and identify the incorrect use of dissonance in the following example.

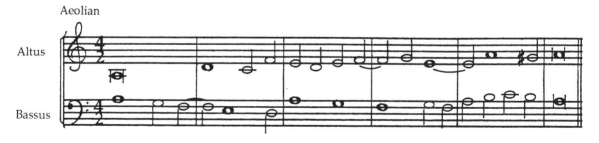

4. Write a countermelody in the Altus that includes half-note passing tones.

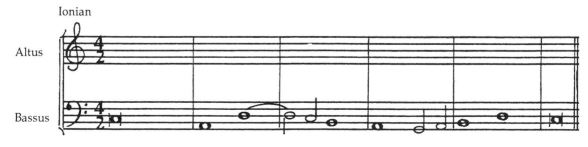

5. Complete the following suspensions.

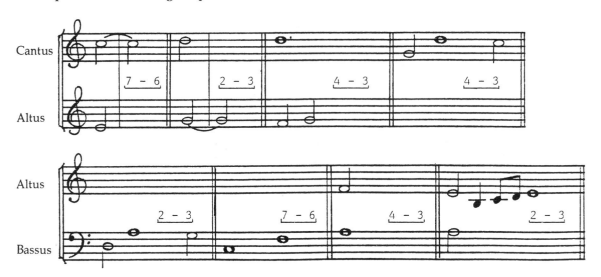

6. Write an example that includes suspensions and half-note passing tones. Use a ⌐7 – 6⌐ or a ⌐2 – 3⌐ suspension on the last accented beat before entering the final.

Worksheet (W–4)
Two-Part Counterpoint

1. Write two measures of imitation beginning on beat one of measure two in the Tenor.[1]

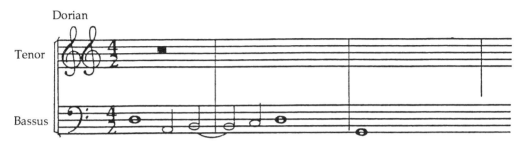

2. Begin imitation in the Altus on beat one of measure two.

3. Begin imitation in the Bassus on beat three of the first measure.

4. Begin imitation in the Bassus on beat one of measure two with an alternate type of imitation.

---

[1]The solution to any exercise in imitation may be found by beginning imitation either at the octave, on the dominant, or on the lower fifth of the final.

5. Write a two-measure melody in the Tenor that is imitated in the Altus. Begin imitation on beat three of the first measure.

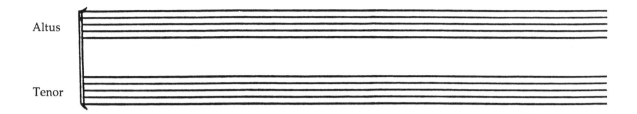

6. Write a two-measure melody that is answered by inversion in the second part.

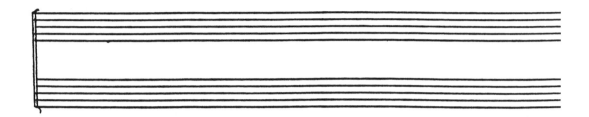

7. Continue the canon in the following example with an additional four measures. Conclude with free counterpoint by adding two measures that includes a ⌐7 – 6⌐ or ⌐2 – 3⌐ suspension on the last accented beat before entering the final.

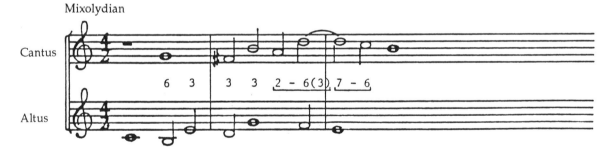

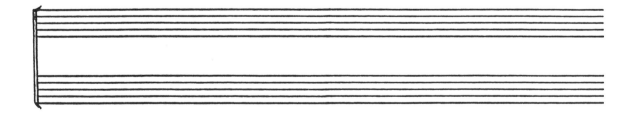

Worksheet (W–5)
Two-Part Counterpoint

1. Write several measures that include examples of accented and unaccented quarter-note passing tones.

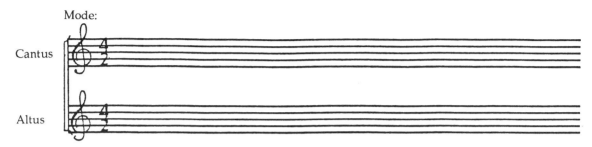

2. Write several measures that include examples of anticipations and (lower) auxiliaries.

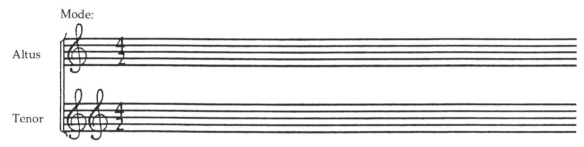

3. Write an example that includes any of the above plus a cambiata and an appoggiatura. Conclude with a suspension that features an ornamental resolution.

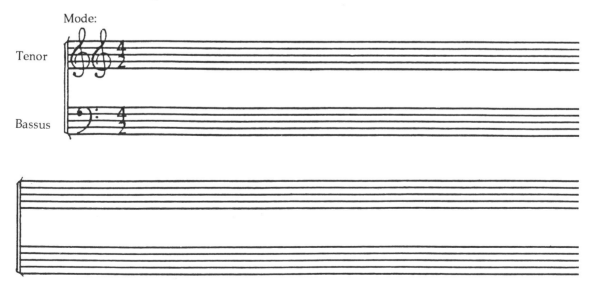

4. Write a two-part exercise that begins with imitation and includes suspensions, half-note passing tones, and black-note dissonances. Conclude with a suspension that leads to the final. Include an interior cadence in this exercise.

5. Write an example similar to Exercise 4 that also includes a text.

Worksheet (W–6)
Three-Part Counterpoint

1. Study the following for voice leading, doublings, and chord quality. Then, notate on separate staves for Cantus, Altus I, and Altus II; also, add an intervallic analysis.

Ionian

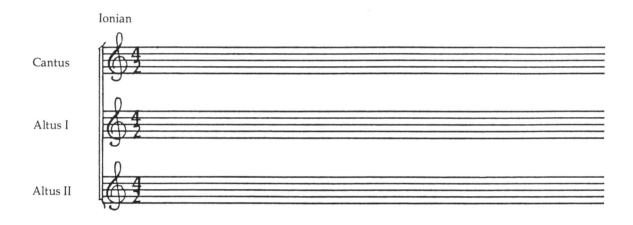

Cantus

Altus I

Altus II

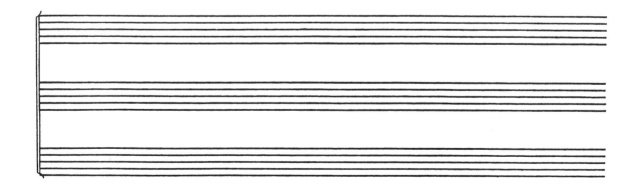

2. Write a three-part exercise similar to Exercise 1 using consonances only.

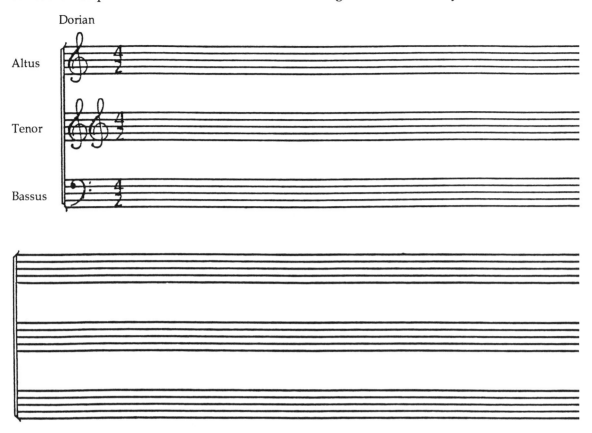

3. Add stepwise half notes wherever indicated (by X) and encircle those that are dissonant.

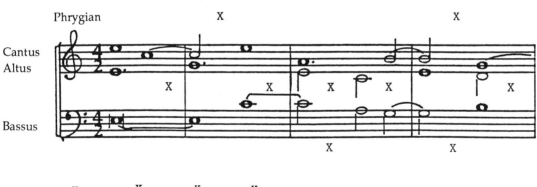

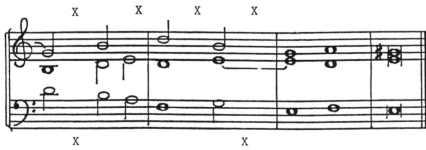

Worksheet (W–7)
Three-Part Counterpoint

1. Rewrite the following for Cantus, Altus, and Bassus. Beginning with measure two, insert half-note passing tones wherever melodic skips of a third occur.

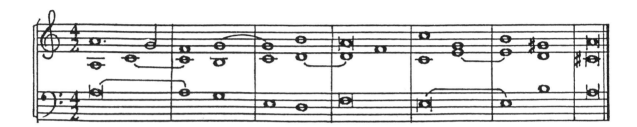

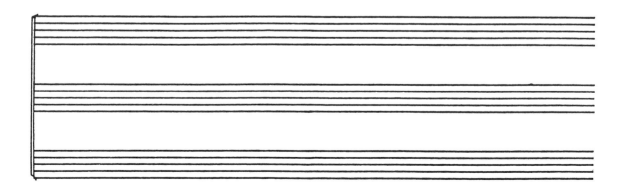

2. Write an exercise for Cantus, Altus, and Tenor using all white-note values. Distribute note values equally among the parts and identify all half-note passing tones with an X.

Worksheet (W–8)
Three-Part Counterpoint

1. Complete the following suspensions in three parts.

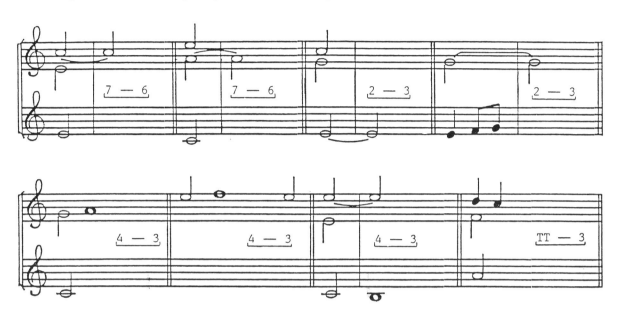

2. Write a short example that includes a $\lfloor 4 - 3 \rfloor$, a $\lfloor 7 - 6 \rfloor$, and a $\lfloor 2 - 3 \rfloor$ suspension.

3. Write an example that includes half-note passing tones and several suspensions. Use a
   ⌞4 – 3⌟ suspension on the last accented beat before entering the final.

Worksheet (W–9)
Three-Part Counterpoint

1. Complete the following by imitating the given subject.

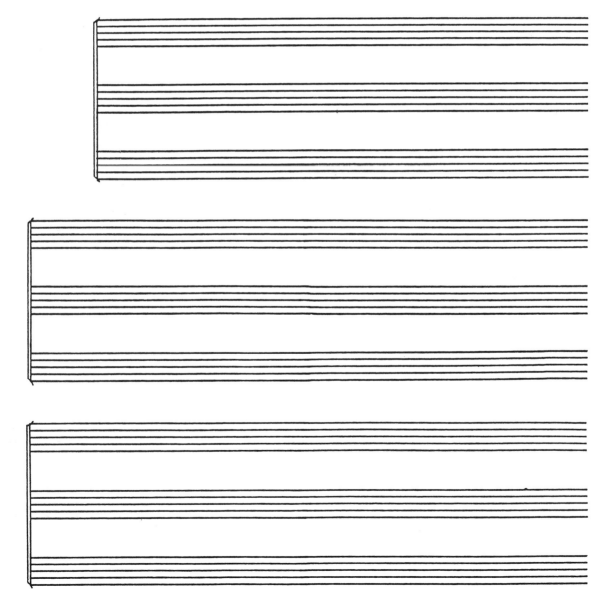

2. Write an exercise that includes suspensions, half-note passing tones, and various quarter-note dissonances. Begin with imitation and use a ⌊4 – 3⌋ suspension on the last accented beat before entering the final.

Worksheet (W–10)
Three-Part Counterpoint

1. Write an exercise similar to Exercise 2 of Worksheet W–9, but this time with text. Use interior cadences to divide the phrases of the text.

Worksheet (W–11)
Four-Part Counterpoint

1. Harmonically analyze (by chord name) measures 16–22 of *Litaniae Liber Secundus*, *Kyrie eleison*, page 181. Study the voice leading and rhythmic setting of the text. Rewrite the phrase to the given harmonic scheme. Use the same text and rhythm as the Altus throughout all the parts.

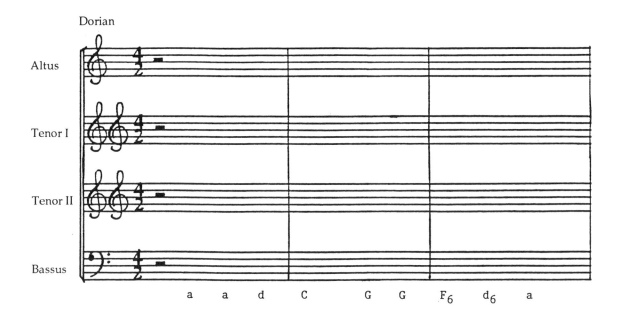

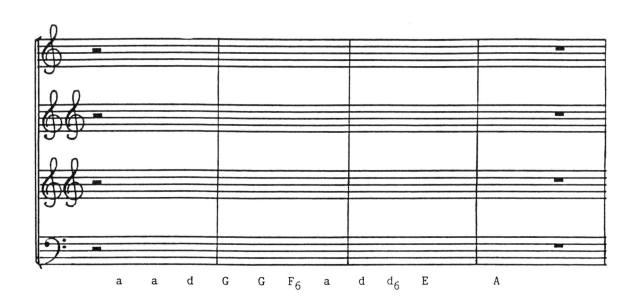

2. Referring again to Litaniae Liber Secundus, write a passage similar to the first example, but using an original harmonic sequence based on the text and rhythm of the Altus, measures 34–42.

Worksheet (W–12)
Four-Part Counterpoint

1. Write out the following in white-note values (the Altus requires an octave transposition). When completed, compare to *Exaudi Domine*, measures 36–47, pages 126–127.
   Note where black-note activity was used by the composer.

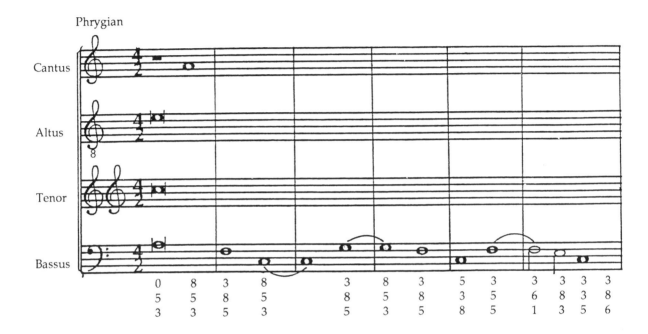

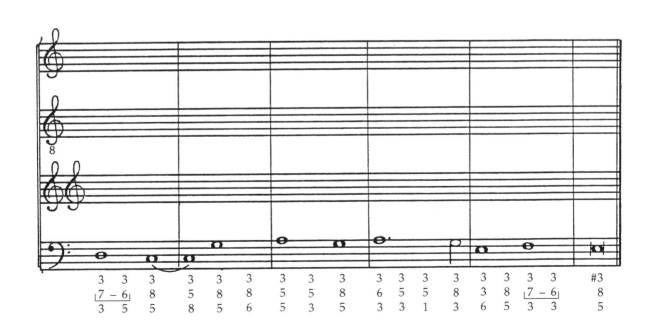

2. List all the possible root-position and first-inversion chords that can be used with the following bass line. The first and last chords should always be written in root position.

3. Write several four-part versions with this bass, using some black-note activity and several suspensions. It may be desirable to work these exercises on two staves at first, but the final copy should be notated on separate staves.

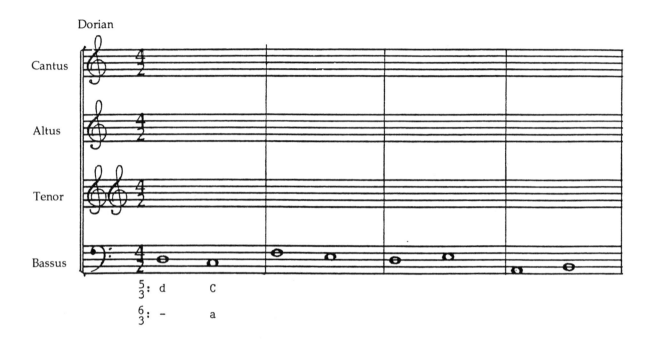

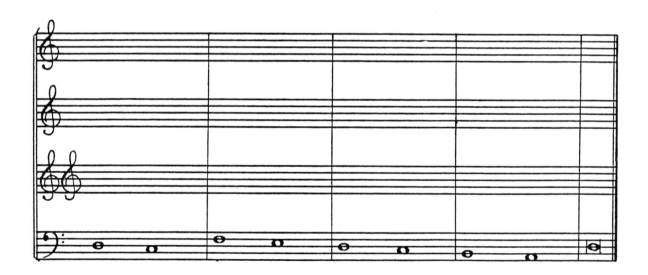

Worksheet (W-13)
Four-Part Counterpoint

1. With a given melody in any part above the bass, each note may serve as the root, third, or fifth of either a root-position or first-inversion chord. List these possibilities as shown below. First complete the Bassus, followed by the Altus and Tenor. Write suspensions where indicated, by an X, and use half-note passing tones wherever suitable. Remember to give preference to root-position chords.

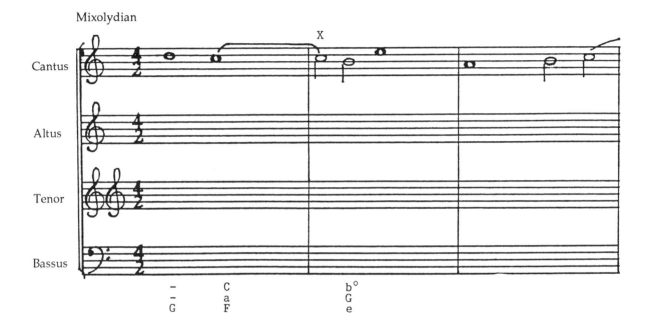

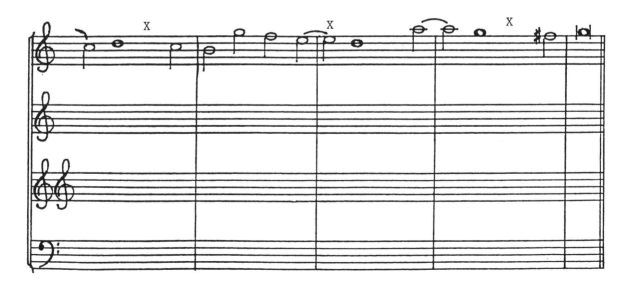

2. As in the preceding example, list the possible chords that may be used with the given Tenor part. Use half-note passing tones and suspensions wherever possible.

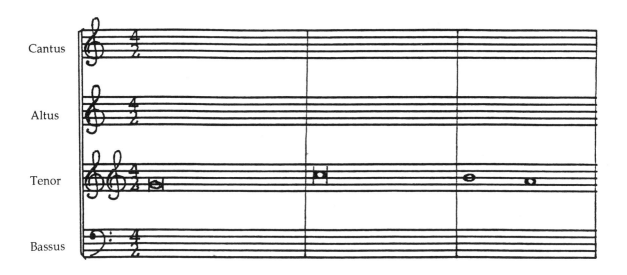

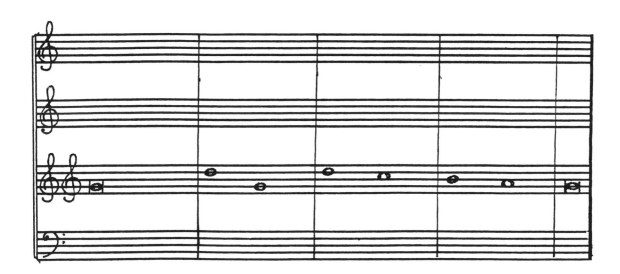

Worksheet (W-14)
Four-Part Counterpoint

1. Add 6–10 measures to the following and conclude with a plagal cadence.[2] Include suspensions, half-note passing tones and black-note dissonances.

---

[2]This imitative subject is taken from Palestrina's Missa: *Ad Fugam, Credo: Et incarnatus est.*

Worksheet (W–15)
Four-Part Counterpoint

1. Write a short motet for four voices with text. Begin with imitation and include suspensions, half-note passing tones, and black-note dissonances.

Selected Bibliography

Basset, Leslie. *Manual of Sixteenth Century Counterpoint.* New York: Appleton-Century-Crofts, 1967.

Benjamin, Thomas. *The Craft of Modal Counterpoint: A Practical Approach.* New York: Schirmer Books, 1979.

Brandt, William, et al. *The Comprehensive Study of Music.* 4 vols. New York: Harper & Row, 1980.

Davidson, Archibald and Apel, Willi. *Historical Anthology of Music.* Vol. 1 (revised edition). Cambridge: Harvard University Press, 1959.

Fux, Johann Joseph. *The Study of Counterpoint.* Translated and edited from *Gradus ad Parnassum*, 1725 by Alfred Mann. New York: W. W. Norton & Co., Inc., 1965.

Gauldin, Robert. *A Practical Approach to Sixteenth-Century Counterpoint.* Englewood Cliffs: Prentice-Hall, Inc., 1984.

Hardy, Gordon, and Fish, Arnold. *Music Literature: A Workbook for Analysis.* Vol. 2 (Polyphony). New York: Dodd, Mead, and Co., 1967.

Jeppesen, Knud. *Counterpoint: The Polyphonic Vocal Style of the Sixteenth Century.* Translated by Glen Haydon. Englewood Cliffs: Prentice-Hall, Inc., 1939.

Krenek, Ernst. *Modal Counterpoint in the Style of the Sixteenth Century.* London: Boosey and Hawkes, 1959.

Mann, Alfred. *The Study of Fugue.* New York: W. W. Norton & Co., Inc., 1965.

Merritt, Arthur T. *Sixteenth-Century Polyphony.* Cambridge: Harvard University Press, 1939.

Morley, Thomas. *A Plain and Easy Introduction to Practical Music.* Edited by R. Alec Harman. New York: W. W. Norton & Co., Inc., 1966.

Morris, R. O. *Contrapuntal Technique in the Sixteenth Century.* New York: Oxford University Press, 1922.

Owen, Harold. *Modal and Tonal Counterpoint.* New York: Schirmer Books, 1992.

Palisca, Claude V. *Norton Anthology of Western Music.* Vol. 1. New York: W. W. Norton & Co., Inc., 1980.

Smith, Charlotte. *A Manual of Sixteenth-Century Contrapuntal Style.* Newark: University of Delaware Press, 1989.

Soderlund, Gustave F. *Direct Approach to Counterpoint in Sixteenth-Century Style.* Englewood Cliffs: Prentice-Hall, Inc., 1947.

Soderlund, Gustave, and Scott, Samuel. *Examples of Gregorian Chant and Sacred Music of the Sixteenth Century.* Englewood Cliffs: Prentice-Hall, Inc., 1971.

Swindale, Owen. *Polyphonic Composition.* London: Oxford University Press, 1962.

Index